NEW PRACTICE READERS

THIRD EDITION

BOOK F

DONALD G. ANDERSON

Associate Superintendent, Retired
Oakland Public Schools
Oakland, California

Phoenix Learning Resources
New York • St. Louis

NEW PRACTICE READERS
THIRD EDITION
BOOK F

Project Management and Production: Kane Publishing Services, Inc.
Cover Design: Pencil Point Studios
Text Design: Craven and Evans, Inc.

ISBN 0-7915-2122-2

3 4 5 6 7 8 9 0

TO THE TEACHER

This book is one of a seven-book series. It is intended to provide reading interest along with comprehension skill development for readers who need additional practice material to achieve mastery. The controlled reading level of each book makes it possible to assign students to the text most suitable for individual reading comfort. Readabilities for this book are 5.4–6.5, consistent with the Dale-Chall Readability Formula.

This book contains nine groups of articles in units labeled A–I. The subjects cover major content fields. The pattern is as follows:
1. Birds
2. Health and natural phenomena
3. Fish and the sea
4. Metals, minerals, chemistry
5. Airflight and industry
6. Numbers and measurements
7. Places and people
8. Language
9. Miscellany

Before each reading selection, there is a readiness activity to introduce difficult words. Teacher supervision at this point will be helpful to later success.

Following the factual articles, there are tests designed to improve specific skills for study reading. Charts at the end of the book provide a place for individual records of progress on each skill.

The six basic skills tested are consistent with those which appear on widely accepted reading achievement tests. In Book F, they are:

1. Implied details. The answer here must be selected from among a group of possibilities. The correct answer is a reasonable conclusion (not one stated in the article) from ideas contained in the reading material. Answering and discussing such questions will give the student valuable experience in reasoning.

2. Meaning of the whole. These questions require that the pupil select the answer which best describes the central theme of the article.

3. Recognition of antecedents. The pupil must show that he or she knows which word or group of words is referred to by such common pronouns as **they, some, it, who, those, this,** and **each**.

4. Determining whether a given idea has been stated affirmatively, negatively, or not at all within the reading matter. This question requires a recognition of the difference between assumptions, however reasonable, and evidence.

5. Awareness of the falseness of a statement in relation to the selection.

6. Recognition of the meaning of a word in context.

At the conclusion of each unit of nine articles, there is a longer story prepared for recreational reading. Many of these stories come from folktales and are intended as pleasure reading and as a basis for group discussion. The *Thinking It Over* questions following each story may be used to launch the discussion or for written practice.

All the selections may be used to develop reading speed where desired. Students should be urged to increase their speed only in terms of their individual results.

A sample exercise precedes the regular lessons. Directions explain the procedure. Ideally, the teacher will work through the sample exercise with the group as a whole.

Read-along cassettes to help the most dependent students are available for Books A, B, C, and D.

TABLE OF CONTENTS

Sample	A Highly Prized Stone	vi
A-1	Standing Still in Midair	4
A-2	A Delicate Matter	6
A-3	A Tiny Engineer	8
A-4	Liquid Silver	10
A-5	At the Mercy of the Winds	12
A-6	The Powers of a Woman	14
A-7	Worldwide Wanderers	16
A-8	Life without Words	18
A-9	Carriers and Passengers	20

A Toast to the South 22

B-1	A Proud Strutter	24
B-2	A Huge Tail	26
B-3	Fish Facts	28
B-4	False Copper	30
B-5	Ships in the Air	32
B-6	Good Pay?	34
B-7	Few Poor, Few Rich	36
B-8	Growing Language	38
B-9	Against the Darkness	40

The Long Struggle 42

C-1	Birds in Dress Suits	44
C-2	A Three-Minute Supply	46
C-3	Stars in the Ocean	48
C-4	Worker Diamonds	50
C-5	An Early Industry	52
C-6	The Search for a Calendar	54
C-7	No Longer Dying Out?	56
C-8	Before Written Language	58
C-9	The End of Knighthood	60

McGoogle and the Lambs 62

D-1	"What an Appetite!"	64
D-2	Bark Medicine	66
D-3	A Shocking Fish	68
D-4	Light but Strong	70
D-5	"Blamed If They Ain't Flew!"	72
D-6	Time from the Stars	74
D-7	Frost and Fire	76
D-8	Thousands of Languages	78
D-9	Breadfruit	80

Wings on His Feet 82

E-1	One Hundred Eyes	84
E-2	Facts about Clouds	86
E-3	A Watery Nest	88
E-4	Metal from the Ocean	90
E-5	Wool Producers	92
E-6	How Many Stars?	94
E-7	It Will Blow Past You	96
E-8	Idea Signs	98
E-9	A Royal Present	100

How Buck Saved His Master 102

F-1	Talking Birds	104
F-2	Nature's Lights	106
F-3	Undersea Cowhands	108
F-4	Garbage Is Big Business	110
F-5	Escape Through the Air	112
F-6	Think Big!	114
F-7	The Rich Coast	116
F-8	Writing without an Alphabet	118
F-9	Camel of Tibet	120

The Electra Mystery 122

G-1	Long-Necked Birds	124
G-2	Skeleton Islands	126
G-3	How Are They Like Us?	128
G-4	Not a Lead Pencil	130
G-5	Soda, Lime, and Sand	132
G-6	Keeping Secrets	134
G-7	Coffee Riches	136
G-8	The First Alphabet	138
G-9	A Nurse but Not a Doctor?	140

Sir Gawain's Marriage 142

H-1	Good or Bad?	144
H-2	Nature's Electric Lights	146
H-3	Glass Fish	148
H-4	The Earliest Metal	150
H-5	Mail by Air	152
H-6	A Convenient Measure	154
H-7	More than Magic	156
H-8	Early Alphabets	158
H-9	Floating Rocks	160

A Powerful Grin 162

I-1	Bird Luck	164
I-2	Blood of the Wrong Color?	166
I-3	A Deadly Fish	168
I-4	Better than Gold	170
I-5	Paper, Paper, Everywhere	172
I-6	True-False	174
I-7	A Giant Artist?	176
I-8	Alpha and Beta	178
I-9	The Firebird	180

Wanted: $12,000 Reward 182

v

HOW TO USE THIS BOOK

There are three parts to each lesson.
1. Questions to help you get ready.
   Read them. Write the answers.

Getting Ready to Read

SAY AND KNOW	
artificial	Draw a line under each right answer or fill in the blank.

artificial

necklace

craftspeople

carve

jewelry

jewelers

gem

emerald

exceptional

1. Something made by people that looks like something natural is
exceptional   artificial   jewelry.

2. Those who make or sell jewels are   gems   jewelry   jewelers.

3. Another word for **jewel** is   craftspeople   gem   necklace.

4. Something not common is   artificial   carving   exceptional.

5. A bright green color may be called   emerald   gem   jewelry.

6. It means **to cut.** _____

---

2. A story to read.

Sample   A Highly Prized Stone

Jade is a gem that was first brought to Europe by Spanish explorers who found it in Central and South America and Mexico. In China, however, jade had been highly prized long before that.

The Chinese have prized

pieces of pure emerald jade above all other gems. For many hundreds of years, they have made things of jade. Among these are good-luck pieces, buttons, rings, hairpins, artificial flowers, necklaces, flutes, bells, and jars. Skilled Chinese craftspeople have long been able to carve jade into the shapes of butterflies, bees, and other animals. They have even learned to carve beautiful pictures on pieces of jade small enough to be worn as jewelry.

Throughout the years, much false jade has been used in place of the real stone. Jewelers can tell real jade by its slightly oily feel, its hardness, and its partly clear look. Although most people think of jade as green in color, it may be orange, light purple and gray, or black and white as well. Bright red and bright yellow jade have also been found, but these types are so exceptional that they are almost never seen.

3. Questions to tell how well you read.
   Read them. Write the answers.
   Put the number you got right in the box.

Sample   Testing Yourself   **NUMBER RIGHT**

Draw a line under each right answer or fill in the blank.

1. While not directly stated, it can be reasoned from the article that
   a. jade is harder than coal.   b. jade is found in Africa.
          c. jade is found in or near China.

2. This article as a whole is about
   a. China.   c. jade.
   b. emeralds.   d. craftspeople at work.

3. The word **it** in the first sentence refers to _____.

4. Eskimos use jade for making bowls.   Yes   No   Does not say

5. Which two sentences are not true?
   a. Real jade is partly clear.   c. Jade is too hard to carve.
   b. Jade feels somewhat oily.   d. Jade is prized in China.
          e. Jade was brought to Europe from North America.

6. What word in the second paragraph means **people who make things by hand?**

1

Answers for the Sample

Check your work. If you made a mistake, find out why. Count your number right and mark the score on your paper.

Getting Ready	Testing Yourself
1. artificial	1. c
2. jewelers	2. c
3. gem	3. jade
4. exceptional	4. Does not say
5. emerald	5. c, e
6. carve	6. craftspeople

Keeping Track of Your Progress

At the back of this book, on page 186, there are record charts. Turn to the charts and read the directions. After you finish each lesson, record your score. Keep track of how you are doing on each type of question.

If you may not mark in this book, make a copy of the charts for your notebook.

NEW PRACTICE READERS

READERS

THIRD EDITION

BOOK F

Getting Ready to Read

Draw a line under each right answer or fill in the blank.

1. **Being able** means **being**   capable   unique   barely.

2. **Movements from one place to another as seasons change** are   migrations   nectars   abilities.

3. **Gets into** means   extracts   unique   penetrates.

4. It is **an act requiring skill.**   barely   feat   migration

5. It means **scarcely** or **only just.**   barely   annually   ability

6. **Basic skills** are _____.

A-1   Standing Still in Midair

The tiny hummingbird is the best flyer of all birds. The hummingbird is capable at any time of flying straight up in the air, flying backwards, and moving its wings so rapidly that it can remain in one spot in the air. Although a hummingbird's wingspread is barely 10 centimeters (4 inches) long on the average, the tiny birds can whiz through the air as swiftly as 96 kilometers (60 miles) an hour. That hummingbirds can travel far as well as fast is shown by the migrations that hummingbirds make annually between the United States and Central and South America.

The hummingbird uses its unique abilities in flying to good advantage. When it locates a honeysuckle vine, for example, it flies straight up and "stands still" in the air in front of a flower. It then directs its long bill into the blossom, which has a deep cup. Moving slowly, the bird flies forward until its bill penetrates the flower's cup to the very bottom. After drinking the nectar it finds there, the hummingbird performs another unique feat: it extracts its bill from the deep flower by flying backwards.

A-1   Testing Yourself

NUMBER RIGHT

Draw a line under each right answer or fill in each blank.

1. While not directly stated, it can be reasoned from the article that
   a. hummingbirds cannot walk.   b. birds fly backwards to rest.
        c. some birds have a wingspread of over 10 centimeters.

2. This article as a whole is about
   a. hummingbird nests.   c. a rare bird.
   b. hummingbird eggs.   d. a bird with special abilities.

3. The word **it** in the last paragraph, second sentence, refers to

   _____.

4. The hummingbird can fly faster than any other bird.   Yes   No   Does not say

5. Which two sentences are not true?
   a. Hummingbirds cannot fly straight up.   c. Some birds fly backwards.
   b. Hummingbirds drink nectar.   d. Hummingbirds are small.
        e. Hummingbirds cannot fly very far.

6. What word in the last paragraph means **draws out?** _____

Getting Ready to Read

SAY AND KNOW

normal
delicate
temperature
variations
probably
regulation
continuous
process
automatically
glands
perspiration
evaporates
reversed

Draw a line under each right answer or fill in the blank.

1. It means **without stopping.**   delicate   continuous   process

2. **Done without thought or attention** means **done**
                              with regulation   automatically   reversed.

3. **Something of the usual type** is considered
                              as variations   a process   normal.

4. It means **the degree of heat.**   **glands   temperature   probably**

5. Water that becomes steam   **perspires   evaporates   reverses.**

6. **Sweat** is the same as _____.

A-2   A Delicate Matter

The normal body temperature of a fully grown person measures about 37° on a Celsius thermometer (98.6°F). Although the body's temperature may vary above and below this point, the variations usually are quite small. A change in the body's temperature of more than 6°C (10°F) either way would probably cause death.

The regulation of body temperature is a delicate and continuous process. In humans and other warm-blooded animals, temperature is automatically kept uniform under normal conditions. In the body, heat is produced at all times, but at varying rates of speed. The heat is carried by the blood to the skin surfaces. From there, it passes off into the air.

If the body becomes too warm, the surface blood vessels become larger and carry more blood. In this way, more heat can be brought to the surface of the skin and sent out of the body. In addi-

tion, as the body becomes warmer, the sweat glands pour out perspiration, which evaporates and helps cool the body.

These processes are reversed when the body becomes cold. To keep the body temperature from dropping far below the normal, the surface blood vessels grow smaller and perspiration is checked.

A-2 Testing Yourself

Draw a line under each right answer or fill in each blank.

1. While not directly stated, it can be reasoned from the article that
   - a. perspiring is harmful.
   - b. body temperature never changes.
   - c. the blood serves the body as a transportation system.

2. This article as a whole is about
   - a. medicine.
   - b. science.
   - c. the body's heating and cooling system.
   - d. how we can regulate body temperature.

3. The word **it** in the second paragraph, fifth sentence, refers to

   _____.

4. Increased perspiration cools the body.   Yes   No   Does not say

5. Which two sentences are not true?
   - a. The body produces heat.
   - b. Body heat should always be 35°C.
   - c. Body heat changes are usually slight.
   - d. We perspire when we are too cold.
   - e. Surface blood vessels get bigger when the body gets too warm.

6. What word in the second paragraph means about the same as **not changing?**

   _____

Getting Ready to Read

SAY AND KNOW

Draw a line under each right answer or fill in the blank.

observed

fiddler

developed

burrow

surrounded

recedes

resembles

orchestra

derives

1. **Looks like** means   **observes**   **resembles**   **derives.**

2. **One who plays a violin or fiddle** can be called

                a burrow   **an orchestra**   **a fiddler.**

3. **Moves back** means   **resembles**   **recedes**   **develops.**

4. It means **the same as grew.**   **developed**   **orchestrated**   **derived**

5. One who **watched carefully** has

                burrowed   **surrounded**   **observed.**

6. **Gets from** means _____.

A-3   A Tiny Engineer

We were not able to build underwater until we could make an airtight box to sink beneath the surface. This kind of box is called a *caisson.* Yet if we had observed the habits of a small sea animal called the fiddler crab, we might have developed and used caissons years sooner.

The fiddler crab, which is only about 3¾ centimeters (1½ inches) wide, lives in a burrow in the sand or mud just below the high-water mark. Each burrow is surrounded by a mound of sand. When the tide is out, the crab sits outside its home or looks for food. About 15 minutes before the incoming tide reaches its door, the crab crawls back into its home and pulls sand into the entrance. In this way, as when people use caissons, air is trapped inside the burrow and water is kept out. About 15 minutes after the tide recedes, the crab pushes away the sand and comes out.

A male fiddler crab has one large claw, which is as wide as his body. When he stands on his hind legs and waves the claw in the air, he resembles the fiddler in an orchestra and, thus, derives his name.

A-3 Testing Yourself

Draw a line under each right answer or fill in each blank.

1. While not directly stated, it can be reasoned from the article that
   a. people cannot live without air.   b. fiddler crabs do not need air.
   c. people cannot build things underwater.

2. This article as a whole is about
   a. caissons.
   b. an animal engineer.
   c. crabs that live on land.
   d. fiddlers.

3. The word **we** in sentence three refers to _____.

4. The fiddler crab eats only plants.   Yes   No   Does not say

5. Which two sentences are not true?
   a. Fiddler crabs are under 4 centimeters across.
   b. All crabs live above the high-water mark.
   c. This crab lives in a burrow.
   d. Crabs need air.
   e. No one knows why the fiddler crab was so named.

6. What word in the second paragraph means **a doorway or a space through which**

   to enter? _____

9

Getting Ready to Read

substance
ancient
Hindus
valuable
explosives
scientific
apparatus
occasionally
sulfur
electrical
expands
contracts

Draw a line under each right answer or fill in the blank.

1. **Very old** means   **Hindus   ancient   valuable.**

2. **Once in a while** means   **scientific   apparatus   occasionally.**

3. **Something of worth** is   **scientific   valuable   ancient.**

4. **Equipment used for a certain kind of work** is called
                                   sulfur   apparatus   contracts.

5. **Matter** or **material** are other words for
                                   substance   electrical   explosive.

6. **The opposite of grows smaller** is _____.

A-4   Liquid Silver

Mercury is the only metal that keeps its liquid form at normal temperatures. It is possible to pour mercury from one vessel to another in exactly the same way that it is possible to pour water. Because of this, people for a long time were not certain that mercury was a true metal. The silver-white substance was known to the ancient Chinese and Hindus. It has been found in Egyptian tombs dating back to 1500 B.C. One ancient Greek writer described the metal as "liquid silver," and even today it is often called quicksilver.

Mercury is a very valuable metal. It is used widely in the making of many useful drugs and medicines. Large amounts of mercury

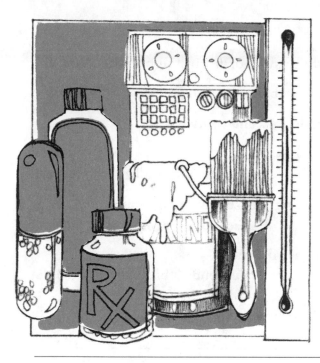

are also used in mixing paints, in making explosives, and in manufacturing electrical and scientific apparatus. Mercury is perhaps most commonly known for its use in thermometers. It is the substance that expands or contracts according to changes in temperature.

Occasionally, mercury is found in its free state among rocks. Most often, however, it is found mixed with sulfur in a beautiful red ore called *cinnabar*.

A-4 Testing Yourself

Draw a line under each right answer or fill in each blank.

1. While not directly stated, it can be reasoned from the article that
   a. mercury is expensive.   b. mercury is used in solid form.
          c. we have learned to separate mercury from sulfur.

2. This article as a whole is about
   a. how mercury was discovered.   c. one use of mercury.
   b. quicksilver.   d. a red ore.

3. The word **it** in the first paragraph, last sentence, refers to

   _____ _____.

4. Mercury is most commonly known for its use in drugs.   Yes   No   Does not say

5. Which two sentences are not true?
   a. Mercury and lead make cinnabar.   c. Mercury is used in thermometers.
   b. Cinnabar is silver in color.   d. Mercury is often found with sulfur.
          e. Quicksilver and mercury are two names for the same metal.

6. What word in the last paragraph means **condition?** _____

Getting Ready to Read

SAY AND KNOW

balloonist

descend

ascend

adverse

mercy

helium

possibility

ballast

barometer

Draw a line under each right answer or fill in the blank.

1. It means **unfavorable** or **bad.**   ballast   barometer   adverse

2. It means **to go up.**   descend   ascend   mercy

3. It is a gas used to make balloons rise.

　　　　　　　　　　　　　balloonist   possibility   helium

4. It tells how high something is by measuring air pressure.

　　　　　　　　　　　　descend   barometer   adverse

5. It is **extra weight carried by a balloon.**

　　　　　　　　　　　ascend   ballast   balloonist

6. What word comes from the word **possible?** _____

A-5   At the Mercy of the Winds

For more than a hundred years, balloonists have tried to fly the Atlantic. One balloonist who tried in 1976 to make the trip alone was Ed Yost. He and his balloon rode the winds from west to east for about four and a half days. But adverse winds caused him to fall short by 1120 kilometers (700 miles).

Balloons are at the mercy of the winds. Whenever Yost found his balloon being blown the wrong way, he would search for a better wind. To do this, he had his balloon go higher or lower. To

ascend, he dropped bags of sand he carried as ballast, making the balloon lighter. To cause the balloon to descend, he let out some of the helium gas.

Yost also had a problem sleeping. To be sure that he woke up whenever the balloon dipped too low, he attached a motorcycle horn to the barometer. The horn blew when the balloon fell to 900 meters (about 3,000 feet).

Yost also had to be careful not to get so high that he might become ill. To guard against this possibility, he regularly inspected his fingernails. Blue nails meant danger

Three men successfully crossed the Atlantic in a balloon in 1978. Finally, in 1984, one man, Joseph W. Kittinger, Jr., crossed the Atlantic in a solo balloon flight covering 5,702 kilometers (3,543 miles). It took him 84 hours.

A-5 Testing Yourself

NUMBER RIGHT

Draw a line under each right answer or fill in each blank.

1. While not directly stated, it can be reasoned from the article that
    a. balloonists trying to cross the Atlantic need winds that blow from north to south.
    b. high-altitude winds often blow in different directions from low-altitude winds.
    c. balloonists must know how to ride bicycles.

2. This article as a whole is about
    a. trying to fly a balloon over the Atlantic.   c. how to find favorable winds.
    b. keeping awake in a balloon.   d. avoiding altitude sickness.

3. The word **he** in the last sentence of the second paragraph refers to _____.

4. Balloons filled with helium are lighter than air.   Yes   No   Does not say

5. Which two sentences are not true?
    a. Ed Yost crossed the Atlantic from America to Europe in a balloon.
    b. Yost was in the balloon for more than four days.
    c. Dropping ballast lets the balloon go higher.
    d. Yost's balloon was filled with hydrogen gas.
    e. Blue fingernails are a sign of poor health.

6. What word in the second paragraph means **to look for?** _____

Getting Ready to Read

Draw a line under each right answer or fill in the blank.

1. **One who is an expert in chemistry** is a

   chemist   computer   comet.

2. It is **a kind of science.**   wizard   physics   astronomer

3. To **investigate carefully** is to do   vitamins   atomic   research.

4. It does math problems quickly.   radioactivity   comet   computer

5. They are necessary for good health.   physics   wizards   vitamins

6. It comes from the word meaning **the smallest particle.**

   _____

A-6   The Powers of a Woman

When Chien-Shiung Wu was honored by Princeton University in 1958 for her research in physics, the audience was warned not to underestimate the powers of a woman.

Grace Hopper served the Navy as a mathematician during World War II. She was a computer expert. In 1985, Grace Hopper was promoted to the rank of rear admiral. She was 79 years old.

Good scientists are usually also good mathematicians. One great scientist was Marie Curie. She, her husband, and her daughter studied radioactivity.

Two famous astronomers were Maria Mitchell and Nancy

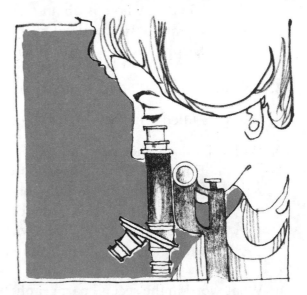

Roman. Mitchell discovered a new comet in 1847. She was the first woman ever to be voted into the American Academy of Arts and Sciences. Roman, called a "wizard in math" while in college, has worked with rockets and space exploration.

Maria Mayer won a Nobel Prize in 1963 for work in atomic science. Later, Dorothy Hodgkin also won a Nobel Prize as a chemist studying vitamins. On June 18, 1983, Sally K. Ride became the first U.S. woman in space. Women are right at home in science labs, in computer research, in mathematics, and even in space!

A-6   Testing Yourself   NUMBER RIGHT

Draw a line under each right answer or fill in each blank.

1. While not directly stated, it can be reasoned from the article that
   a. all women are good in mathematics.
   b. there is no reason why women cannot do well in mathematics.
   c. women do not like mathematics and sciences.

2. This article as a whole is about
   a. women who are good with math.   c. women who are astronomers.
   b. computers used by the Navy.   d. Princeton University.

3. The word **she** in the third sentence, fourth paragraph, refers to

   _____.

4. All good mathematicians are good scientists.   Yes   No   Does not say

5. Which two sentences are not true?
   a. Chien-Shiung Wu was a physicist.
   b. Nancy Roman discovered a new comet in 1847.
   c. Grace Hopper was in the Navy.
   d. Maria Mitchell was an expert on vitamins.
   e. Maria Mayer won a Nobel Prize.

6. What word in the second paragraph means **someone who knows a great deal about something**? _____

15

Getting Ready to Read

gypsy
wanderers
wandered
unwritten
definitely
originated
century
itinerant
musicians
estimated
refusing

Draw a line under each right answer or fill in the blank.

1. It is **the opposite of accepting.** **refusing** **itinerant** **century**

2. **Began** means **wandered** **estimated** **originated.**

3. **Not recorded** may mean **gypsy** **unwritten** **definitely.**

4. **Guessed on the basis of some facts** means **unwritten** **estimated** **musicians.**

5. People traveling about may be described as **musicians** **itinerant** **estimated.**

6. **Those who move about without a fixed stopping place** are

_____.

A-7 Worldwide Wanderers

The gypsy people are wanderers whose unwritten history dates back many hundreds of years. Because gypsies have kept no written records, their early history is not definitely known. It is known, however, that Romany, the language of the gypsies, originated in India, and it is probable that the first home of the gypsies was in that country.

Gypsies in large bands roamed through the countries of Asia for many years before any of them migrated to Europe. Some

16

gypsy tribes finally found their way to Europe in the early fifteenth century. Not too long afterwards, gypsies could be found in all parts of the world. They usually lived as itinerant workers, keeping to themselves and, for the most part, refusing to settle in any one place for long. Gypsies became known as fine musicians and metal workers. Many of them also worked as horse traders and fortune-tellers.

Although most gypsies do not mix with the people in the countries through which they wander, they usually speak the language of the people among whom they live.

No one knows how many gypsies there are in the world today, since gypsies live in small groups and avoid census takers. The gypsy population is estimated to be between 1 and 6 million worldwide.

A-7 Testing Yourself

NUMBER RIGHT

Draw a line under each right answer or fill in each blank.

1. While not directly stated, it can be reasoned from the article that
   a. gypsies cannot write.
   b. there is a gypsy language.
   c. the place of origin of the gypsies can only be guessed.

2. This article as a whole is about
   a. fortune-telling.
   b. Romany.
   c. people from India.
   d. gypsies.

3. The words **that country** in the first paragraph, last sentence, refer to

   _____.

4. Gypsy comes from the word Egyptian.   Yes   No   Does not say

5. Which two sentences are not true?
   a. Most gypsies speak English.
   b. Gypsies have their own land.
   c. Gypsies are wanderers.
   d. Romany began in India.
   e. There are between 1 and 6 million gypsies in the world today.

6. What word in the first paragraph means **surely** or **for certain**?

   _____

Getting Ready to Read

SAY AND KNOW

consider

pattern

altered

modern

methods

communication

disappear

depend

elaborate

abandoned

Draw a line under each right answer or fill in the blank.

1. **To think about** is to   alter   consider   depend.

2. **Changed** means   altered   disappeared   abandoned.

3. **Particular ways of doing some things** are
                                   communications   methods   modern.

4. **Given up completely** is   abandoned   patterned   elaborated.

5. **Of the present time** means   elaborate   modern   method.

6. **Giving information by speaking or by writing** is

   _____.

A-8   Life without Words

It has been claimed that without language, it would be impossible for people to live together.   Let us consider how our pattern of life would be altered if we did not have written or spoken language.

Because our modern methods of communication are built directly upon the use of language, these methods would disappear.   We would have no books, newspapers, magazines, telephones, radios, or television.   We would have no schools, libraries, offices, or hospitals.   All of these things depend

upon the use of language. In addition, we would have no modern means of transportation, for the movement of trains, ships, automobiles, and airplanes is based upon written directions and oral communication. Our elaborate exchange of goods would have to be abandoned. Without the help of language, merchants could not sell their goods, and without transportation, they could not get goods to sell.

We suspect that many thousands of years ago, people lived who did not have written or spoken language. How different their world must have been from the one we know! Because no written or spoken language existed, no records of these early times could be kept. We can only imagine how the people who lived without words were able to get along.

A-8 Testing Yourself

NUMBER RIGHT

Draw a line under each right answer or fill in each blank.

1. While not directly stated, it can be reasoned from the article that
   a. civilization depends on language.   b. language is not necessary.
              c. trade does not require language.

2. This article as a whole is about
   a. books and newspapers.   c. the uses of radio.
   b. the importance of language.   d. how people of long ago lived.

3. The word **they** in the second paragraph, last sentence, refers to

   _____.

4. Since life began, people have always had some kind of written language.
                              Yes   No   Does not say

5. Which two sentences are not true?
   a. Transportation needs no language.
   b. Language does not help us.
   c. Communication depends on language.
   d. Language helps people live together.
   e. We know little about the world before written language.

6. What word in the first paragraph means **said?** _____

Getting Ready to Read

SAY AND KNOW

SAY AND KNOW

communication
destination
population
species
billion
estimates
exist
required
advance

Draw a line under each right answer.

1. **The opposite of to go backward** is to   **advance   require   exist.**

2. **Where you are going** is **your**
                                population   communication   destination.

3. It means about the same as **kind.**   **species   billion   estimates**

4. **Careful guesses** are   **species   destination   estimates.**

5. It means the same as **needed.**   **required   advance   population**

6. It is **a thousand million.**   **trillion   billion   population**

A-9   Carriers and Passengers

Pigeons are found in every part of the world except the coldest areas. There are about 290 species. The most interesting of these birds are the carrier pigeons and the passenger pigeons.

Carrier pigeons carried messages as long ago as the days of the Roman Empire. Modern armies, with all their advanced telephones, telegraphs, and radios, still train pigeons to carry messages. When other communications fail, carrier pigeons, which are swift and small, are likely to arrive safely at their destination.

The other interesting pigeon is one that no longer exists.

Martha, the last passenger pigeon on Earth, died September 1, 1914, in a zoo in Cincinnati. At one time, there were more passenger pigeons on Earth than any other kind of bird. Estimates of the number of these birds in the 1860s went as high as 9 billion. This is more than twice the human population

of the Earth 100 years later. Yet now there are none.

Hunters killed thousands of pigeons at a time. They were sold as food for 2 cents each. Their feathers were used for bed stuffing. Just one mattress required the feathers of 144 dozen birds. Now there will never be another passenger pigeon.

A-9 Testing Yourself

NUMBER RIGHT

Draw a line under each right answer or fill in the blank.

1. While not directly stated, it can be reasoned from the article that
   a. a mattress required the feathers of over 1500 passenger pigeons.
   b. carrier pigeons are so small they are never shot down.
   c. the only way Roman armies had for delivering messages was by carrier pigeon.

2. This article as a whole is about
   a. hunters of pigeons.
   b. two kinds of pigeons.
   c. armies and pigeons.
   d. a bird that no longer exists.

3. The word **they** in the last paragraph, second sentence, refers to

   _____ .

4. The greatest number of pigeons is found in the hottest countries.

   Yes   No   Does not say

5. Which two sentences are not true?
   a. There were more passenger pigeons than human beings at one time.
   b. Martha was the last of the carrier pigeons.
   c. Martha died in a zoo early in this century.
   d. Passenger pigeons were good to eat.
   e. Some pigeons may be found near the North Pole.

6. What word in the first paragraph means **regions?** _____

A Toast to the South

Pauline Cushman was not afraid to die. She knew the penalty for spying. But she hoped she would not be hanged by the Confederates. She preferred to be shot like a soldier.

As she lay ill in prison, she thought of her life before the Civil War. She had been born in New Orleans, but the family had soon moved to Michigan.

At 18, she had become an actress. Soon she was playing leading roles. Then the war began.

One night, she startled her audience. Her part called for her to toast the Union. Instead, she changed the lines to say, "Here's to the South!" Her listeners gasped, but they guessed that, since she had been born in the South, her sympathies lay there.

The truth was that a Southern officer had challenged her to change the toast. Loyal to the Union, she secretly reported the incident to Northern officers. They recognized that she had an unusual chance to help the Northern cause. Because she was born in the South and because of the toast she made, she would likely be accepted in the South. She could travel among Southern troops and collect information for the North. She agreed and was commissioned as a secret agent.

She then crossed the battle lines into the South. She pretended to look for her brother, a Southern officer. She rode from camp to camp gathering information. Southerners loyal to the North helped her send back the information. Sometimes, her letters were mixed in flour, baked into bread, and smuggled north.

But one day, she was caught with the plans of Fort Shelbyville hidden in the sole of her boot. Now she awaited the court martial's verdict, hoping she was not to hang.

As the officer came into her cell, she looked anxiously at him. "What is my fate? Am I to hang?" The officer's face told her the answer.

"I am sorry. You are to be hanged in ten days." Pauline Cushman sank back on her cot, resigned to her worst fears.

The days passed, too quickly. The Confederate doctor attending her tried to console her.

Meanwhile, Union troops nearby were rapidly approaching. The Confederates had to move, but could their sick prisoner be taken along?

It was then that the Confederate doctor said Pauline was too ill to be moved. He predicted she would die within a mile if they attempted to take her. Possibly he believed what he said. Or maybe he and the other officers did not want to see the young woman hang.

Whatever the reason, the Confederates hastily retreated but left Pauline Cushman behind. Eventually she returned to the North and was greeted and praised by President Abraham Lincoln.

MY READING TIME _____ **(456 WORDS)**

Thinking It Over

1. Why do you think Pauline Cushman preferred to be shot rather than hanged?

2. Why are spies executed rather than being kept prisoner like ordinary soldiers?

3. Do you think the Confederate doctor was telling the truth when he said Pauline was too ill to be moved?

Getting Ready to Read

SAY AND KNOW

strutting
magnificent
glistening
composed
glorious
plumage
crest
pheasant
ornaments
curiosities
captivity
thrive
commonly

Draw a line under each right answer or fill in the blank.

1. **Walking in an important way** is called

            strutting   glistening   glorious.

2. **To grow strong** means **to**   compose   magnificent   **thrive.**

3. **A tuft of feathers on a bird's head** is **its**

            curiosities   captivity   **crest.**

4. **Grand** or **splendid** means   plumage   **magnificent**   commonly.

5. It is **a bird used for food.**   **pheasant**   plumage   ornaments

6. **Rare** and **strange objects** are _____.

B-1   A Proud Strutter

One of the most beautiful sights in the bird world is the male peafowl, or peacock, strutting proudly about with its magnificent tail raised and its richly colored tail feathers glistening in the sunlight.

24

The peacock's many-colored "tail" is not really a tail at all. It is a fan composed of stiff, beautiful feathers. This fan is supported by the peacock's true tail. In addition to the glorious plumage, a peacock has a crest of upright feathers on its head. The peahen, or female peafowl, has no such grand coloring. Instead, the peahen is usually colored a dull brown and has neither fan nor crest.

The peafowl is a member of the pheasant family. It may be found living wild in the jungles of Asia and of the East Indies. Tame peafowl may be seen in nearly all other parts of the world, where, although their flesh and their eggs are both good for table use, they are generally kept as ornaments or curiosities in parks and in zoos.

Peafowls in a wild state feed on grass, grain, frogs, insects, and snails. In captivity, however, they thrive on grains commonly fed to poultry.

B-1 Testing Yourself

NUMBER RIGHT

Draw a line under each right answer or fill in each blank.

1. While not directly stated, it can be reasoned from the article that
   a. peahens are not vain.   b. peacocks are sometimes white.
   c. it is easy to tell peacocks from peahens.

2. This article as a whole is about
   a. the pheasant family.   c. a kind of pheasant.
   b. the peacock's tail.   d. the foods birds eat.

3. The word **they** in the last sentence refers to _____.

4. The peacock's many-colored fan holds up its true tail.   Yes   No   Does not say.

5. Which two sentences are not true?
   a. The peahen's fan has 24 feathers.   c. Peafowl are good to eat.
   b. Wild peafowl eat grain and grass.   d. Peacocks have crests.
   e. Peafowl may be found wild in most parts of the world.

6. What word in the first paragraph means about the same as **shining?**

25

Getting Ready to Read

SAY AND KNOW

orbit
rare
interval
streak
solid
portion
celestial
atmosphere
extend
appearance
benefit
knowledge
ancestors

Draw a line under each right answer or fill in the blank.

1. **To move in a path around something** is to

                                     orbit   **streak**   **benefit.**

2. **Celestial** means **having to do with**   **earth**   **sky**   **water.**

3. **The air around the earth** is called **the**

                         ancestors   **atmosphere**   **interval.**

4. **Not happening often** means   **appearance**   **rare**   **solid.**

5. **Time between** means   **interval**   **knowledge**   **portion.**

6. **To stretch out** means to _____.

B-2   A Huge Tail

A comet is a heavenly body with a long tail. Comets orbit about the sun. At rare intervals, a comet may be seen from Earth, appearing as a streak of light that travels swiftly across the heavens.

The head of a comet contains a more or less solid portion called the nucleus. The comet's tail, however, contains so little solid matter that Earth or another planet could pass through it without any harmful effects. Even if one of the largest comets were to strike Earth head on, we would notice only a shower of meteors. These meteors are hot celestial bodies entering the atmosphere of Earth at great speeds.

It is hard, therefore, for us to imagine that the head of a comet may be over a million kilometers

26

wide and that a comet's tail may extend over 100 million kilometers in space!

In ancient times, the appearance of a comet aroused great alarm among people. It was believed that a comet would be followed by some great misfortune. Such fear is not surprising. Without benefit of scientific knowledge, our ancestors had no way of knowing the natural causes of such an object.

B-2   Testing Yourself

NUMBER RIGHT

Draw a line under each right answer or fill in each blank.

1. While not directly stated, it can be reasoned from the article that
   a. there are comets in the universe that cannot be seen from Earth.
   b. a large comet is a common sight.
   c. misfortunes in ancient times were largely caused by comets.

2. This article as a whole is about
   a. why people fear comets.   c. comets and how they act.
   b. the history of comets.   d. the heavenly bodies.

3. The word **it** in the second paragraph, second sentence, refers to

_____ _____.

4. Comets used to be larger than those today.   Yes   No   Does not say

5. Which two sentences are not true?
   a. The head may be very wide.   c. The nucleus contains solids.
   b. Comets are natural things.   d. The tail is made of heavy material.
      e. A very large comet hitting Earth might destroy the planet.

6. What word in the last paragraph means **bad luck?**

_____

Getting Ready to Read

actually
characteristics
identified
obtains
oxygen
various
transmit
definite
inhabit
opportunity
certain

Draw a line under each right answer or fill in the blank.

1. To live in means   **to inhabit**   **obtains**   **to transmit.**

2. Chance means   **oxygen**   **opportunity**   **characteristics.**

3. Recognized as being the same means
                              identified   **certain**   **obtained.**

4. Different means   **definite**   **various**   **certain.**

5. Really means   **opportunity**   **definite**   **actually.**

6. One gas without color or smell is named _____.

B-3   Fish Facts

Many people use the word *fish* to describe any animal that lives in the water. Many water animals, however, are not actually fish. A real fish has particular characteristics by which it can be identified. For example, a real fish has a back-

28

bone. It obtains air by means of gills, which are slits placed one on either side just behind the head. It has fins that assist it in swimming. In addition, a real fish may also be identified by the way it breathes. Water enters a fish's mouth and passes out through its gills. The gills remove oxygen from the water, and the blood carries this oxygen to various parts of the fish's body.

Fish are interesting animals. They have a well-developed sense of hearing, and are able to receive and to transmit sound. For the most part, fish do not swim about without plan or purpose. Different kinds of fish live in definite places. Even if fish are taken away from the areas they naturally inhabit, they will try to return when the opportunity is presented.

Scientists, through experiments, have shown that fish are capable of learning and can be taught to act in certain ways.

B-3 Testing Yourself   NUMBER RIGHT

Draw a line under each right answer or fill in each blank.

1. While not directly stated, it can be reasoned from the article that
    a. animals cannot live in water.   b. fish have no lungs.
    c. real fish have no skeletons.

2. This article as a whole is about
    a. why fish blush.   c. fish and their characteristics.
    b. fish sleeping and listening.   d. fish and other water animals.

3. The word **they** in the second paragraph, last sentence, refers each time to

_____ .

4. Fish can hear better than most animals.   Yes   No   Does not say

5. Which two sentences are not true?
    a. Not all water animals are real fish.   c. We know that fish can hear.
    b. Deep-sea fish have no backbones.   d. Fish do not need oxygen.
    e. Fins help a fish to swim.

6. What word in the first paragraph means about the same as **help** or **aid**?

_____

Getting Ready to Read

SAY AND KNOW

associate
yield
combined
combination
withstanding
strain
alloys
stainless
chromium
corrodes

Draw a line under each right answer or fill in the blank.

1. **Eats away slowly** means   **yields**   **corrodes**   **associates.**

2. **Something that will not rust** is called

           alloys   **combinations**   **stainless.**

3. **Joined together** means   **strained**   **withstanding**   **combined.**

4. **To connect ideas in thought** means **to**

           chromium   **alloy**   **associate.**

5. **Hard use** can cause   **yield**   **combination**   **strain.**

6. **Holding up under** means _____.

B-4   False Copper

Many people associate a metal called nickel with the five-cent piece of the same name. This

coin, however, is composed three-fourths of copper and one-fourth of nickel.

Nickel is a silver-white, shining substance found in an ore that closely resembles copper ore. Because the ore did not yield copper as they expected, people who first found it called the metal it did yield *kupfernickel*, or false copper.

Nickel is a metal that corrodes slowly. Because of this, it is widely used for coating other metals, such as steel, to protect them from rust. Nickel is also used in combination with other metals to make mixtures called alloys. For example, nickel and chromium may be combined with steel to produce stainless steel. Nickel and steel may be combined to produce nickel steel, a substance capable of withstanding much strain. Most of the world's nickel supply is used to manufacture nickel steel.

Only a small amount of nickel is produced in the United States. Large amounts of the metal are imported to the United States each year from Canada, which, along with the former Soviet Union, mines most of the world's nickel supply.

B-4 Testing Yourself

NUMBER RIGHT

Draw a line under each right answer or fill in each blank

1. While not directly stated, it can be reasoned from the article that
    a. copper has more value than nickel.
    b. nickel's chief value is its ability to combine with other metals.
    c. nickel alloys do not rust easily.

2. This article as a whole is about
    a. how alloys are made.
    b. the uses of nickel.
    c. the uses of alloys.
    d. copper and nickel.

3. The word **it** in the second paragraph, second sentence, refers both times to

_____.

4. The United States uses large amounts of nickel.   Yes   No   Does not say

5. Which two sentences are not true?
    a. Nickel does not rust easily.
    b. *Kupfernickel* means copper.
    c. Canada supplies much nickel to the world.
    d. Nickel and steel alone make stainless steel.
    e. The coin named nickel is made mostly of copper.

6. What word in the third paragraph means **able?** _____

Getting Ready to Read

Draw a line under each right answer or fill in the blank.

1. A machine that never gets out of order is

                                               reliable   gondola   rigid.

2. The back of a ship is **its**   rigid   gondola   stern.

3. The part that steers a ship is a   propeller   rudder   stern.

4. It means **very sad.**   reliable   tragic   fin

5. It is **like a skeleton.**   framework   fin   rudder

6. If it is **firm** or **not bending,** it is _____.

B-5 Ships in the Air

Balloons cannot provide reliable transportation because they must go where the winds blow them. Airships, however, can be steered.

Airships and balloons are both lighter than air, being filled with helium gas. But an airship, unlike a balloon, has motors to provide power, and rudders and fins for steering.

Airships are of three kinds. A nonrigid ship is usually called a blimp. It has no metal ribs or backbone. A semirigid ship has a backbone from bow to stern. A rigid airship has a light framework of aluminum rings and girders. It is divided into 12 to 16 separate balloons. One of these balloons can be deflated without hurting the others.

Each of the three kinds of airships has five parts. First is the bag holding the helium gas. Second is the car, called a gondola, for the passengers. Third are propellers to force the ship through the air. Fourth are the motors, that turn the propellers. Finally, there are the rudders to steer the ship up or down, left or right.

Airships have made many long flights in past years. But there have also been a number of tragic accidents. As a result, interest in airships has decreased.

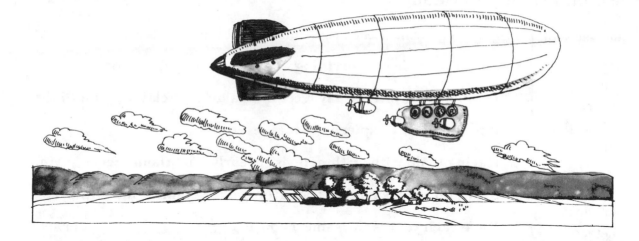

B-5 Testing Yourself

Draw a line under each right answer or fill in each blank.

1. While not directly stated, it can be reasoned from the article that
   a. balloons are useful for carrying cargo.
   b. a rigid airship is safer than nonrigid or semirigid airships.
   c. helium lifts airships better than hydrogen.

2. This article as a whole is about
   a. balloons and the wind.   c. helium gas.
   b. ships that are lighter than air.   d. the five parts of every airship.

3. The words **the others** at the end of the last sentence of the third paragraph refer to

   _____.

4. Helium is safer than hydrogen for airships.   Yes   No   Does not say

5. Which two sentences are not true?
   a. A gondola carries people.
   b. A blimp is a semirigid airship.
   c. A balloon can steer itself.
   d. All airships have motors.
   e. All airships have propellers.

6. What word in the third paragraph means **the air has been let out?**

   _____

Getting Ready to Read

Draw a line under each right answer or fill in the blank.

1. It means **whole** or **everything**.   salary   average   total

2. **People who work for pay** receive   **salaries**   **claims**   **methods**.

3. It means **each**.   apiece   average   total

4. **Having to do with arithmetic** is   yearly   mathematical   giving.

5. **A worker who is paid** is   **an average**   **a claim**   **an employee**.

6. **Once each year is the same as once** _____ **year**.

B-6   Good Pay?

The Better Buy Company claims it pays its workers very well. Fifteen people work for the company. The two owners pay themselves $60,000 per year apiece.

Three employees get $40,000 each. There are four who receive $25,500 and six who earn $18,000 apiece.

The total year's pay for the company is $450,000. How can we decide whether the company really does pay well?

One way is to divide the total pay, $450,000, by 15, the number of workers. The answer, $30,000, is what the average worker receives. The mathematical word for this average is *mean*.

But there could be two other answers. We can find what the *middle* pay is. We first list the 15 salaries from largest to smallest. Then we count down from the top to the middle, which is the eighth place. Doing this, we get $25,500. This is the *median*, or middle, pay.

The third way is to ask which pay is given *most often*. Since six workers receive $18,000, and this is more than those receiving other salaries, $18,000 is the answer. This is called the *mode* salary.

The Better Buy Company could have used any of these three methods. Which method do you think they used to make their claim that they pay workers very well?

B-6   Testing Yourself

Draw a line under each right answer or fill in each blank.

1. While not directly stated, it can be reasoned from the article that
   a. it is easy to tell whether the company pays well.
   b. the company probably used the mean, or average, method.
   c. the workers disagreed with the company.

2. This article as a whole is about
   a. salaries of the company owners.
   b. how to figure mean pay.
   c. ways of judging pay.
   d. expenses of the company.

3. The word **themselves** in the third sentence, first paragraph, refers to

   _____.

4. The workers making $25,500 a year thought that the company pays well.

   Yes   No   Does not say

5. Which two sentences are not true?
   a. The company had one owner.
   b. Three workers made $40,000 a year.
   c. The median tells what the middle is.
   d. Twelve workers made less than $30,000 a year.
   e. The total pay for the company for a year was less than $500,000.

6. What word in the first paragraph means about the same as **says** or **argues**?

   _____

Getting Ready to Read

provide
current
moisture
warmth
ample
hydroelectric
quality
replace
chemical

Draw a line under each right answer or fill in the blank.

1. It is **a kind of river in the ocean.**   current   chemical   replace

2. It means **to give** or **to furnish.**   ample   provide   moisture

3. It means **wetness** or **dampness.**   quality   hydroelectric   moisture

4. It describes **electricity from water power.**

                                              warmth   quality   hydroelectric

5. It means **plenty of.**   warmth   current   ample

6. What word comes from the word **chemistry?** _____

B-7   Few Poor, Few Rich

Sweden is a northern country. In size, it is a bit larger than California, stretching about 1600 kilometers (1000 miles) north and south. Much of its ground is frozen the year round.

In spite of the frozen ground, its farms provide almost enough food to feed all the Swedes. One reason is the North Atlantic Drift. The Drift is a warm ocean current which runs from the Gulf of Mexico to the North Atlantic. Winds blowing over this current carry moisture and warmth to Sweden. The current also keeps much of the sea ice-free.

Another reason for Sweden's good crops is that the Swedes are excellent farmers. They have learned to farm scientifically. They have also learned to treat their huge forests like farms. They cut only the number of trees they can replace.

No oil and little coal have been found in Sweden. But many rivers and lakes provide ample water for hydroelectric power for electricity. High-grade iron ore mined in Sweden has resulted in the famous high-quality Swedish steel.

The Swedes are good scientists. More chemical elements have

been discovered by them than by the scientists of any other country.

People live well in Sweden. There are few who are very poor, and few who are very rich.

B-7 Testing Yourself

Draw a line under each right answer or fill in each blank.

1. While not directly stated, it can be reasoned from the article that
   a. Swedish education in science is excellent.
   b. Sweden's trees will all be cut down in a few years.
   c. Sweden will run out of electricity before long.

2. This article as a whole is about
   a. producing electricity in Sweden.
   b. a country about the size of California.
   c. farming in Sweden.
   d. forests in Sweden.

3. The word **them** in the fifth paragraph, second sentence, refers to _____.

4. The ice-free sea allows ships to sail to Sweden all year.   Yes   No   Does not say

5. Which two sentences are not true?
   a. All of Sweden's ground is frozen the year round.
   b. Sweden grows almost all its own food.
   c. Sweden has little coal and oil.
   d. There are no rich people in Sweden.
   e. Sweden is a country in the north.

6. What word in the fourth paragraph means **very well known?**

_____

Getting Ready to Read

SAY AND KNOW

linguists

gestures

attempt

gradually

express

prehistoric

imagine

generation

familiar

verbally

Draw a line under each right answer or fill in the blank.

1. **People who are experts on languages** are

                                   gestures   gradually   linguists.

2. It means **before written history.**   verbally   prehistoric   attempt

3. **To make known** means **to**   imagine   express   attempt.

4. People born about the same time are of the same

                                generation   familiar   gestures.

5. Expressed **verbally** means expressed **in**

                                  gestures   words   thoughts.

6. **To form a picture in the mind** is **to** _____.

B-8 Growing Language

Linguists believe that prehistoric people used many gestures to communicate with one another. Gestures, it is thought, were our first form of communication, and the only one we had for a long period of time. Even today we use some sign language: for example, we shake our heads to indicate yes and no, we point, and we wave.

The first spoken words may have been attempts to imitate the sounds made by animals. Then people may have developed sounds of their own. Gradually, people may have repeated certain sounds

so often that the sounds became familiar and understandable to others. Once spoken language had begun, perhaps new words were invented as they were needed for people to express themselves verbally or to name new objects. In this way, we can imagine language growing.

By using words, parents were able to teach them to their children. The children in turn probably made up new ones. Each generation, therefore, in the development of language, knew more words than the generation before it. Language is still growing and changing. Can you think of some words that you use today that were not used by your parents or grandparents when they were children?

B-8 Testing Yourself

Draw a line under each right answer or fill in each blank.

1. While not directly stated, it can be reasoned from the article that
   a. no one is sure of the beginnings of spoken language.
   b. people could always speak.
   c. at one time, people and animals could speak with one another.

2. This article as a whole is about
   a. sign language.   c. parents learning to speak.
   b. new words.   d. how speech may have begun.

3. The word **them** in the last paragraph, first sentence, refers to

   _____.

4. Sign language and spoken language probably appeared at about the same time.
   Yes   No   Does not say

5. Which two sentences are not true?
   a. We use mostly sign language.   c. Children can learn languages.
   b. Language has stopped growing.   d. Animals can make sounds.
      e. Early people probably first used sign language.

6. What word in the second paragraph means **copy?** _____

Getting Ready to Read

SAY AND KNOW	Draw a line under each right answer or fill in the blank.

described
Phoenicia
procedure
material
filtered
petroleum
wax
mentioned
traders
merchandise
tallow

1. Fluid passed through a cloth has been
                                        filtered   mentioned   described.

2. **Things for sale** are   wax   **Phoenicia**   **merchandise**.

3. **Spoken about** means   **procedure**   **traders**   **mentioned**.

4. Most candles are made of   **earth**   **wax**   **petroleum**.

5. **Way of doing things** means   **procedure**   **trader**   **petroleum**.

6. **The stuff of which a thing is made** is the _____.

B-9   Against the Darkness

Blazing pieces of wood were used by early people as their first lights. Later, we learned to make candles for furnishing light. Candles were used to light homes. They were also used elsewhere when small amounts of light were needed. Candles and candlesticks are mentioned in the part of the Bible called the Old Testament, but the material used to make these candles is not described. It is believed that wax candles were invented in ancient Phoenicia. We know that Phoenician traders had wax candles as merchandise as long ago as 2000 years.

The earliest wax candles may have been prepared by dipping a wick into the wax made by bees. We are not sure of this, however, for

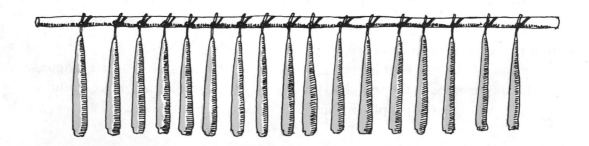

other kinds of wax appear in ancient records. Later, candles were made of animal fat called tallow. In colonial days in America, candles were made by dipping wicks into hot tallow, cooling them, and dipping them again. This procedure was repeated until the candles were thick enough for use.

Today candles are used mostly as decorations and are usually made by machinery. The material used is a wax that has been filtered out of petroleum and refined.

B-9   Testing Yourself   NUMBER RIGHT

Draw a line under each right answer or fill in each blank.

1. While not directly stated, it can be reasoned from the article that
      a. tallow candles were made quickly.   b. cave dwellers used candles.
              c. candles were used before the Christian Era.

2. This article as a whole is about
      a. early candles.   c. the history of candles.
      b. early ways of lighting.   d. the development of lighting.

3. The word **that** in the last sentence refers to _____.

4. Egyptians were probably the first people to use wax candles.
                         Yes   No   Does not say

5. Which two sentences are not true?
      a. The Bible described candles of wax.   c. Burning wood gives light.
      b. Machines are used to make candles now. d. Once candles were of tallow.
              e. Candles today are needed for giving light.

6. What word in the first sentence means **burning?** _____

A Long Struggle

Over a hundred years ago, Sarah Winnemucca was a little Paiute tribe girl in Nevada. When she saw a white settler for the first time, she was afraid. When she was older, she knew that she had been right to fear some white people. Some of them took Native American lands. Some stole furs from forest traps. Sometimes they shot Native Americans just for sport.

But Sarah also knew there were good white people. Her grandfather, Chief Winnemucca, moved her family to California when she was young. There, Sarah learned to speak English and Spanish. She started school, but she was allowed to attend for only 3 weeks. Some of the white children's parents objected to her.

In 1860, the Paiutes were put on a Nevada reservation where the agent in charge cheated them. Sarah's baby brother, her mother, and her sister died. The starving Paiutes begged for food from the Army. Sarah, speaking English, did the talking. The Army helped them.

Next the tribe was moved to a reservation in Oregon. Again the agent cheated. Another tribe on the reservation, the Bannocks, decided to fight. Sarah's father and some other Paiutes wished to remain at peace. But they were forced to join the Bannocks.

The tribes lost the battle. They were all ordered, Bannocks and Paiutes together, to a reservation in the state of Washington. Sarah asked that the Paiutes not be forced to go. She knew that the Bannocks were angry at them for not wishing to fight. Her begging was useless. It was the dead of winter. Overcoats were given to the men. The women received nothing. Many people froze to death on the long, hard trip. Worst of all, when they arrived, they found that only the Bannocks had been expected. No food, clothing, or shelter was ready for the Paiutes!

Desperately, Sarah decided to go to the government office in San Francisco to tell their story. The people there paid to send her to Washington, D.C. In Washington, she told President Rutherford Hayes the story. He promised help. But

the orders he had written out were ignored.

Sarah would not give up. She wrote a book about the Paiutes. She asked people to sign a petition. Thousands did so. Finally, Congress passed a bill ordering the government to keep its promises. But again nothing happened.

Three years later, the brave Paiute woman was dead. She was worn out by her long, unsuccessful fight for her people.

MY READING TIME _____ **(450 WORDS)**

Thinking It Over

1. In what ways do you think some agents on the reservations might have cheated the Native Americans?

2. Do you think the Paiutes were right to try to keep peace?

3. Was Sarah Winnemucca's life a failure?

Getting Ready to Read

SAY AND KNOW

usually

maintain

erect

posture

comical

amusing

fashion

alternate

upright

remainder

Draw a line under each right answer or fill in the blank.

1. **A position of the body** is called **a**

   fashion   remainder   posture.

2. **Something standing up straight** is

   upright   amusing   usually.

3. **Something funny** is   **erect   comical   fashion.**

4. **To take turns** is **to   maintain   alternate   posture.**

5. Something amusing usually causes us to   **laugh   cry   shout.**

6. **That part which is left over** is called **the**

   _____ .

C-1   Birds in Dress Suits

Interesting birds called penguins live around the South Pole. These birds usually spend all their waking hours in the water. Only during the egg-laying and mating periods do penguins actually live on land. Yearly, as mating time draws near, the penguins swim to their breeding grounds and gather in huge flocks.

During the egg-laying period, the female penguin lays usually one egg. This egg is kept in a flap of skin, much like a pocket, located near the top of the penguin's feet. The male and female penguins alternate in caring for the egg. After the baby penguin is hatched, its mother cares for it until it is able to walk. Then it joins the other babies, and the whole group is watched by a few adults, leaving the remainder of the flock free to hunt for food.

Penguins commonly are black with black heads and white breasts. Large penguins often stand about a meter (3 feet) in height. Since a penguin's legs are placed far back, it is able to maintain a very erect posture. It is amusing to watch penguins and to see how much the upright birds resemble humans in dress suits walking in a comical fashion.

C-1 Testing Yourself

Draw a line under each right answer or fill in each blank.

1. While not directly stated, it can be reasoned from the article that
   a. penguins find their food in water.
   b. penguins wear clothes.
   c. penguins swim better than they fly.

2. This article as a whole is about
   a. an amusing polar bird.
   b. the King Penguin and its young.
   c. sea birds in cold lands.
   d. exploring the Antarctic.

3. The word **it** in the second paragraph, last sentence, refers to

   _____.

4. Penguins spend most of their time on land.   Yes   No   Does not say

5. Which two sentences are not true?
   a. Penguins sometimes live in flocks.
   b. Penguins have white backs.
   c. Penguins stand 2 meters tall.
   d. Penguins usually lay one egg.
   e. Penguins take good care of their young.

6. What word in the third paragraph means about the same as **look like?**

   _____

Getting Ready to Read

Draw a line under each right answer or fill in the blank.

1. As much food as is needed would be

                                          storage   adequate   digestion.

2. Very actively means   **activities   strenuously   fortunately.**

3. To gain means **to   acquire   hamper   intestines.**

4. Something full-grown is   **digestion   adequate   adult.**

5. Hampered means   **held back   helped   agreed with.**

6. Something being kept for future use is being kept in

_____.

C-2   A Three-Minute Supply

The body of the average adult has in storage enough food to last for several weeks. It has enough water to last for several days. At any one time, however, the body has only enough oxygen stored in the lungs to last for 3 or 4 minutes! Fortunately, it is not difficult for us to acquire the oxygen we need. As a rule, we need only to breathe in the air around us for an adequate supply.

The amount of oxygen needed at any one time depends upon what

the person is doing. As the activities of the body increase, the use of oxygen also increases. The person begins to breathe deeper and faster to bring more oxygen into the lungs.

More red cells are thrown into the bloodstream to aid in carrying the added supply of oxygen. Blood from the stomach and the intestines is transferred into the blood vessels of the muscles that are at work. This blood helps to transfer the added oxygen to the parts of the body that need it.

It is best not to exercise strenuously right after eating. If blood is transferred from the stomach right after a meal, digestion of food will be hampered.

C-2   Testing Yourself

NUMBER RIGHT

Draw a line under each right answer or fill in each blank.

1. While not directly stated, it can be reasoned from the article that
       a. oxygen is stored for future use.   b. violent exercise is bad.
       c. a ball player will probably use more oxygen than a librarian.

2. This article as a whole is about
       a. the way we breathe.   c. oxygen in the body.
       b. red blood cells.   d. why exercise is sometimes harmful.

3. The word **it** in the second paragraph refers to _____.

4. The more slowly we breathe, the more oxygen we take in.
           Yes   No   Does no say

5. Which two sentences are not true?
       a. Red blood cells carry oxygen.   c. We can do without water for days.
       b. Exercise makes us breathe faster.   d. We can do without oxygen for days.
       e. A person uses about the same amount of oxygen at all times.

6. What word in the first paragraph means about the same as **get?**

_____

47

Getting Ready to Read

creature
unusually
spiny
protection
haunt
suitable
secured
diet
partial
shallow
star-shaped

Draw a line under each right answer or fill in the blank.

1. **The opposite of commonly** is   **unusually**   **suitable**   **spiny.**

2. **A place which you visit often** may be called **your**
            diet   **haunt**   **suitable.**

3. It means **not deep.**   **suitable**   **shallow**   **unusually**

4. **Held fast** means   **protection**   **creature**   **secured.**

5. **Something that is right for a certain purpose** is called
            shallow   **spiny**   **suitable.**

6. **The usual food of a person or animal** is his or her _____.

C-3   Stars in the Ocean

One of the most interesting animals to be found in the sea is a star-shaped creature called a starfish. The most common type of starfish has a round body from which five long arms extend. In the center of the body is the starfish's mouth, which opens into its unusually large stomach. At the end of each arm is a small, colored spot called an eye. A starfish is covered with tough, spiny skin, and extra spines grow around each eye for added protection.

Starfish are sometimes found in pools, but their favorite haunt is on the ocean floor in shallow water. There the starfish crawl or glide by using many small feet. These feet can be pushed out through holes on the underside of each arm. Each small foot has a sucker on the end. By using the suckers, the starfish is able to fasten its feet to some suitable object. Then, with one part of its body secured in this way, it can pull the rest of the body after it.

The diet of a starfish is composed of clams, mussels, snails, and other small sea creatures. It is most partial, however, to oysters.

C-3 Testing Yourself

Draw a line under each right answer or fill in each blank.

1. While not directly stated, it can be reasoned from the article that
     a. the starfish is smart.   b. the starfish is well named.
                          c. the starfish can swim.

2. This article as a whole is about
          a. the food of the starfish.   c. different kinds of starfish.
          b. the body of the starfish.   d. the starfish's body, habits, and food.

3. The word **it** in paragraph two refers each time to _____.

4. Starfish like best to stay on the ocean floor.   Yes   No   Does not say.

5. Which two sentences are not true?
          a. The starfish eats snails.
          b. The starfish has five arms.
          c. The starfish has five eyes.
          d. The starfish has a shell instead of skin.
          e. The starfish is usually found on the top of the ocean.

6. What words in the last paragraph mean **likes best?** _____

Getting Ready to Read

Draw a line under each right answer or fill in the blank.

1. **Unnecessary** is **the opposite of**   **precious**   **essential**   **vast.**

2. It means **very large.**   **worthless**   **vast**   **glittering**

3. **Of no use** means   **unchanged**   **essential**   **worthless.**

4. Thinking about something in connection with something else is thinking about it   **preciously**   **essentially**   **relatively.**

5. Anything that is **useful** is   **practical**   **glittering**   **evidence.**

6. **Things that belong to you** are **your**_____.

C-4   Worker Diamonds

Glittering gems called diamonds are among the most precious of human possessions. Through the ages, they have been a lasting evidence of wealth. Lands may lose their soil, buildings may be destroyed, stocks and bonds may become worthless, but the value of diamonds remains relatively unchanged.

Diamonds are not of value only as signs of wealth. In addition, the diamond is the hardest, longest-wearing substance known. Because

of this, it is very valuable for practical use. In fact, about three-fourths of the total annual supply of diamonds is used in factories and machine shops.

A diamond in the end of a cutting tool can cut through the hardest steel, but only a diamond can cut another diamond. Because of their unusual hardness, diamonds are used to sharpen grinding wheels. They are placed on the tips of the grinding drills used to cut through tons of bedrock. In scores of other ways, diamonds are essential to turning the wheels of modern machinery.

About 56 million industrial diamond carats are mined annually (181.81 tons). The vast diamond mines of South Africa and Zaire produce a lot of these diamonds, but in recent years many industrial diamonds have also come from Russia and Australia.

C-4   Testing Yourself   **NUMBER RIGHT**

Draw a line under each right answer or fill in each blank.

1. While not directly stated, it can be reasoned from the article that
   - a. diamonds are found in the earth.
   - b. diamonds used in industry wear out and must be replaced.
   - c. only small diamonds are used in industry.

2. This article as a whole is about
   - a. industrial diamonds.
   - b. polishing diamonds.
   - c. diamonds as lasting wealth.
   - d. the qualities and uses of diamonds.

3. The word **they** in the third paragraph, third sentence, refers to

   _____.

4. Only steel will cut a diamond.   Yes   No   Does not say

5. Which two sentences are not true?
   - a. Diamonds can cut steel.
   - b. Diamonds are used in industry.
   - c. Industry uses 1/4 of our diamonds.
   - d. Australia supplies some diamonds.
   - e. Many things are known to be harder than diamonds.

6. What work in the first paragraph means **highly prized** or **costly**?

   _____

Getting Ready to Read

SAY AND KNOW Draw a line under each right answer or fill in the blank.

anchored
lassos
synthetic
fibers
twisted
hemp
native
handmade
types
lofty

1. **Kinds** means   **native**   **handmade**   **types.**

2. **Very high** means   **lofty**   **anchored**   **handmade.**

3. **Something that belongs to a certain place** is called
       hemp   **native**   **handmade.**

4. **Long ropes ending in loops** are   **lassos**   **types**   **fibers.**

5. Nylon and rayon are   **anchors**   **hemp**   **synthetics.**

6. Something **turned** or **wound** is _____.

C-5   An Early Industry

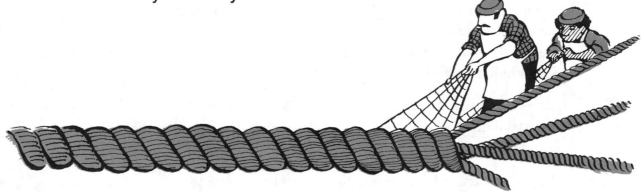

The mention of rope may suggest fishers pulling in their nets, lofty sailing ships being anchored, or huge loads being lifted. It may also bring to mind children playing jump-rope games and cowhands swinging their lassos.

Rope is a common article and is one of the most useful things ever devised. No one knows who first learned to make it, but we do know that ropemaking of one sort or another was one of the world's earliest industries. People of long ago made rope from the fibers of certain plants, from the bark of trees, and from animal hides cut into strips and twisted. Today most rope is made of several kinds of hemp, especially from Manila

52

hemp, or from sisal fibers. The hemp plant, a native of Asia, is now also grown in Europe and America. The strongest rope today is made of synthetic fibers, such as nylon and rayon.

Long ago, all rope was made by hand. Even the great cables that were used on sailing vessels in the early days were handmade. In 1820, the first factory for making rope was built. Today almost all types of rope are made by machinery in factories.

C-5 Testing Yourself

NUMBER RIGHT

Draw a line under each right answer or fill in each blank.

1. While not directly stated, it can be reasoned from the article that
  a. rope is a very, very old invention.
  b. rope made in factories is not as good as rope made by hand.
  c. steel cables have taken the place of rope for many uses.

2. This article as a whole is about
  a. materials used to make rope. c. the importance of cables.
  b. the history of making rope. d. ropes used by children.

3. The word **it** in the second sentence refers to _____.

4. Hemp rope is stronger than sisal rope. Yes No Does not say

5. Which two sentences are not true?
  a. Nylon rope is very strong. c. Rope is a recent product.
  b. A rope factory was built in 1820. d. Rope once was made from hides.
    e. Rope was first made from plant fibers after 1820.

6. What word in the first sentence means **bring to a person's mind?**

Getting Ready to Read

search
employed
precisely
periodically
correct
eventually
construct
scheme
revised
revisions
placement

Draw a line under each right answer or fill in the blank.

1. One who is **hired** is   employed   revised   searched.

2. **A plan** is a   revision   scheme   placement.

3. **To build** is to   correct   employ   construct.

4. **Exactly** means   periodically   eventually   precisely.

5. **Corrected or changed forms** may be called
                                    revisions   placements   schemes.

6. The word that means **in the end** or **finally** is

_____.

C-6   The Search for a Calendar

No calendar that people have employed so far has been precisely accurate. The Roman calendar, which was like the Babylonian calendar, used 12 months of 30 days each. It had to be corrected periodically by the addition of an extra month. Eventually this calendar became so confused that Julius Caesar, leader of Rome, decided to construct a new one.

Caesar based his calendar on 365¼ days, planning to have 6 months with 30 days and 6 months with 31 days. This scheme, however, yielded 366 days. To correct

54

this, Caesar took 1 day from February, which the Romans considered the last month of the year, reducing the number of days in February to 29.

Other revisions were later made until this "Julian" calendar

had, like ours, 7 months with 31 days, 4 months with 30 days, and February with 28 days. To account for the extra ¼ day, every fourth year was made a leap year with 366 days.

In 1582, Pope Gregory XIII made some changes in this calendar. With other minor revisions, this is the one we still use today. It will keep the dates in their proper placement until about the year 4000, when it will have to be revised again.

C-6   Testing Yourself   NUMBER RIGHT

Draw a line under each right answer or fill in each blank.

1. While not directly stated, it can be reasoned from the article that
    a. the division of the year has always been the same.
    b. the number of days in the year is always the same.
    c. no calendar will ever be exactly right.

2. This article as a whole is about
    a. the Roman calendar.   c. the development of the calendar.
    b. why calendars are wrong. d. the revised Julian calendar.

3. The word **one** in the first paragraph refers to _____.

4. Our present calendar should be accurate until the year 4000.

                                            Yes   No   Does not say

5. Which two sentences are not true?
    a. Our calendar is permanently right.   c. Julius Caesar made a calendar.
    b. Babylonians used a 12-month   d. No calendar is wholly accurate.
       calendar.
    e. Pope Gregory XIII revised the Julian calendar in the fifthteenth century.

6. What word in the first paragraph means **mixed up?** _____

55

Getting Ready to Read

SAY AND KNOW

Asiatic

descent

peaceable

flexible

initially

occupied

occupation

population

approximately

decreased

extinct

census

increase

Draw a line under each right answer or fill in the blank.

1. **Something that gets larger** has begun to

    increase   decrease   descent.

2. **The opposite of warlike** is   population   flexible   peaceable.

3. **To die out** is **to become**   flexible   initially   extinct.

4. **An official count** is   **an increase**   **an occupation**   **a census.**

5. The word that means **nearly** or **about** is

    occupied   initially   approximately.

6. **The opposite of grew bigger** is _____.

C-7   No Longer Dying Out?

Extending westward from Alaska almost to the Asiatic coast is a chain of islands called the Aleutian Islands. Almost all of these belong to the United States, having been included when the United States bought Alaska from Russia in 1867.

The people who live on these islands took their name from the islands and called themselves Aleuts. Many of the Aleuts today are of mixed descent, being partly Russian.

The Aleuts speak their own language and live in a quiet, peaceable manner. The men hunt and fish from kayaks. The women are noted as the makers of fine baskets, which they weave by hand and which are very flexible.

When the Russians initially occupied Alaska in the 18th century, the Aleut population totaled approximately 25,000. During the period of occupation, however, their number decreased. In 1945, there were only about 1,400 of them and the Aleut were thought to be nearly extinct. However, the 1960 census listed about 6,000 Aleuts, and the 1990 census listed almost 12,000. This increase in number indicates the Aleuts are now a growing and thriving people.

C-7   Testing Yourself

NUMBER RIGHT

Draw a line under each right answer or fill in each blank.

1. While not directly stated, it can be reasoned from the article that
   a. the Aleuts still weave baskets.
   b. the number of Aleuts grew during Russian occupation.
   c. the Aleuts did not adjust well to the Russian occupation.

2. This article as a whole is about
   a. the Aleutian Islands.
   b. a peaceable island people.
   c. fishing from kayaks.
   d. how the Aleuts make baskets.

3. The word **these** in the second sentence refers to _____.

4. All Aleuts first came from Russia.   Yes   No   Does not say

5. Which two sentences are not true?
   a. We bought Alaska in 1867.
   b. The Aleuts make stiff baskets.
   c. Russia did own the Aleutian Islands.
   d. There were only about 1,400 Aleuts in 1945.
      e. The Aleutian Islands extend eastward from Alaska.

6. What word in the third paragraph means **not stiff**? _____

57

Getting Ready to Read

SAY AND KNOW

analyze

categories

spoken

oral

experiences

notched

reminder

symbolized

certainty

Draw a line under each right answer or fill in the blank.

1. **Things shown by signs** are   **notched**   **spoken**   **symbolized**.

2. **To separate into parts and examine** means
   notched   **to analyze**   **experiences**.

3. **Something to help you remember** is
   oral   **a reminder**   **categories**.

4. **Something said aloud** is   **certainty**   **notched**   **spoken**.

5. **Sureness** means   **certainty**   **symbolize**   **categories**.

6. **Using speech** means **spoken** or _____.

C-8   Before Written Language

People seem to use many different methods to communicate with one another. When we analyze these methods, however, we find that they fall into three main categories. Thoughts and ideas are communicated by means of signs, or sign language; by means of speaking words aloud, or oral language; and by means of writing words, or written language.

Early in the history of the world, people found that they could not communicate well by using only

58

sign language. In some way that we cannot trace with any certainty, they devised spoken language. It was only after the development of oral communication that people began trying to record their messages, their experiences, and their ideas.

Some early messengers carried with them notched sticks. The sender of the message had notched the sticks while telling the message to the messenger. Each notch stood for a part of the message and served as a reminder. Some people also devised systems of knotted strings for keeping records. The knots symbolized different happenings, often births, deaths, and battles. Others used the notched sticks in combination with knotted strings of different lengths and colors that stood for certain things.

C-8 Testing Yourself

NUMBER RIGHT

Draw a line under each right answer or fill in each blank.

1. While not directly stated, it can be reasoned from the article that
   a. a language is never the invention of one person alone.
   b. early people were not interested in keeping records.
   c. there is no way to keep records other than with numbers.

2. This article as a whole is about
   a. methods of communication.   c. sign language.
   b. writing.   d. speech today.

3. The word **they** in the second sentence refers to _____.

4. Much early human speech came from animal sounds.   Yes   No   Does not say

5. Which two of these sentences are not true?
   a. There are four main methods of communication.
   b. Records of the beginnings of spoken language are fairly complete.
   c. Early humans first developed sign language.
   d. Writing came after speaking.
   e. People are able to communicate with one another.

6. What word in the last paragraph means **cut** or **grooved?**

Getting Ready to Read

SAY AND KNOW

generally
published
descriptions
saltpeter
charcoal
proportions
widespread
equipped
muskets
effective
chivalry

Draw a line under each right answer or fill in the blank.

1. **For the most part** means   **widespread**   **generally**   **chivalry.**

2. **Furnished with what is needed** is

          armored   **equipped**   **published.**

3. It is **a white mineral.**   **charcoal**   **muskets**   **saltpeter**

4. **Made public in writing** is   **proportion**   **published**   **armor.**

5. Something that produces the wanted end is

          description   **effective**   **equip.**

6. Word pictures of anything are _____.

C-9   The End of Knighthood

Gunpowder is the oldest of all explosives. After it came into wide use, this invention brought about great changes in history.

No one knows when gunpowder was first made. It is believed, however, that it was used by the Chinese very early in history.

Directions for making gunpowder were not generally known until 1242. In that year, a well-known Englishman, Roger Bacon, published descriptions of the manufacture of gunpowder. In his writings, he said that gunpowder should be made of 41 parts of saltpeter, 29½ parts of sulfur, and 29½ parts of charcoal.

To this day, gunpowder is made from these three things. The proportions in modern times, however, are 75 parts of saltpeter, 15 parts of charcoal, and 10 parts of sulfur.

As the use of gunpowder became more widespread, it brought to an end that period of history called the Age of Chivalry. During that time, the most powerful fighters had been knights equipped with lances, horses, and heavy armor. Knighthood ended when soldiers with muskets were more than equally effective in battle.

C-9   Testing Yourself

Draw a line under each right answer or fill in each blank.

1. While not directly stated, it can be reasoned from the article that
    a. Bacon invented gunpowder.   b. gunpowder could damage armor.
                c. gunpowder was used by knights.

2. This article as a whole is about
    a. the effect of gunpowder on history.   c. the chemistry of gunpowder.
    b. how gunpowder was made.   d. why wars are harmful.

3. The word **it** in the second sentence refers to _____.

4. The Age of Chivalry began with gunpowder.   Yes   No   Does not say

5. Which two sentences are not true?
    a. Gunpowder is made today exactly as it was in Bacon's time.
    b. Charcoal is used in making gunpowder.
    c. Gunpowder ended the Age of Chivalry.
    d. Gunpowder was first used in 1242.
    e. The use of gunpowder is important historically.

6. What word in the last paragraph means **space of time?** _____

McGoogle and the Lambs

Algernon McGoogle was what Westerners call a "dude." For the sake of his health, McGoogle had moved from the East to Happy Valley, Arizona. As soon as he arrived in Happy Valley, McGoogle let it be widely known that he had been on the Yale University track team, and had almost broken the world's record for the hundred-yard dash.

Happy Valley was a center for shearing sheep. Each spring, sheep herders drove their flocks down into the valley. McGoogle was short of cash upon his arrival, and soon he found work as a herder. His job was to herd a flock of sheep among the greasewood and sagebrush on the desert during the day. At night, because of the danger of coyotes, he was to round up his flock and drive it back to the corral.

On the first morning, Reed, the boss, told McGoogle to wander along slowly with his flock and to let the sheep feed as they moved along. He warned the new shepherd to return to the corral by five in the evening. Then, with a mischievous twinkle in his eye, Reed added, "Don't let any of the lambs get away from the flock."

Reed knew that McGoogle probably did not know a lamb when he saw one. And he also knew that there were no lambs in McGoogle's band of sheep.

62

The sheep and their new shepherd soon disappeared into the desert. No one thought of them until supper time. By then, when there was no sign of the runner or his sheep, Reed began to worry a bit. When by seven o'clock they had still not arrived, Reed decided to look for them. Just then, McGoogle and his sheep came into sight. The runner looked very tired. He drove the flock into the corral. Then he wearily dragged himself to the tent. When he saw Reed, he said, "Well, Boss, I'm finished! Back

East I was considered a pretty good foot racer, but I guess I'm not. I'll bet any one of your sheep herders can beat me. Any fellow who can keep track of that band for a week and not lose the lambs could easily break the world's record! I didn't lose any lambs today, but one day of this work is enough for me." McGoogle wiped his forehead. "I ran every one of those crazy lambs back into the band every time they tried to get away. Go and count them and pay me for today. I'm through!"

Reed, knowing there had been no lambs in McGoogle's flock, went to the corral to see for himself. There, huddled off in a corner away from the sheep, he counted 47 jackrabbits and 16 cottontails!

MY READING TIME ⸻ **(450 WORDS)**

Thinking It Over

1. What are some things that make this story funny?

2. Why did Reed want to play a joke on McGoogle?

3. Was McGoogle justified in telling people that he was a good runner? Give reasons for your answer.

Getting Ready to Read

Draw a line under each right answer or fill in the blank.

appetite
exclaim
wholly
succession
enormous
partially
digest
pouch
distributed
assemble

1. **The opposite of very small** is   **wholly**   **partially**   **enormous.**

2. **To gather together** means **to**   **exclaim**   **assemble**   **digest.**

3. **One after another** means   **in succession**   **distributed**   **pouch.**

4. **To change food so the body can use it** is to
   distribute   **appetite**   **digest.**

5. **Desire for food** is called   **pouch**   **enormous**   **appetite.**

6. It means **cry out in surprise.** _____

D-1   "What an Appetite!"

"What an appetite!" one might exclaim upon seeing a pelican in a zoo or a park at feeding time. These birds live almost wholly on fish, and will gobble one after another in rapid succession. The pelicans seem to have enormous appetites indeed. But they are not really eating all the food they take in so rapidly. Pelicans partially digest the fish they swallow and then store the partially digested food in a pouch that is attached to the lower jaw. This pouch is large enough to hold about 4 liters (1 gallon) of liquid. Later the pelican will eat the food stored in the pouch or will share the supply with its young.

Pelicans are large, web-footed water birds, widely distributed in warm regions, and often seen along the shores of seas, lakes, and rivers. The big birds assemble in colonies during nesting or mating time. At such times, there may be thousands of pelicans at one place.

In North America, the eastern brown, the California brown, and the white pelicans are found. The white pelican is the largest of these, sometimes being 1½ meters (5 feet) long and having a wingspread of almost 3 meters (9 feet).

D-1   Testing Yourself

Draw a line under each right answer or fill in each blank.

1. While not directly stated, it can be reasoned from the article that
   - a. pelicans in North America are dying out.
   - b. pelicans eat food only if it is in liquid form.
   - c. young pelicans need help in getting their food.

2. This article as a whole is about
   - a. the pelican's food.
   - b. how pelicans swim.
   - c. where pelicans are found.
   - d. a web-footed water bird.

3. The word **they** in the fourth sentence refers to _____ .

4. Pelicans eat fish.   Yes   No   Does not say

5. Which two sentences are not true?
   - a. Pelicans have webbed feet.
   - b. Pelicans are poor fishermen.
   - c. White pelicans are the smallest kind.
   - d. Pelicans have large pouches.
   - e. Three kinds of pelicans are found in North America.

6. What word in the first paragraph means **quickly?** _____

Getting Ready to Read

SAY AND KNOW

according to
Peruvian
invaluable
treatment
disease
anopheles
tropical
preparations
typhoid
rheumatic
cinchona

Draw a line under each right answer or fill in the blank.

1. A thing of value beyond measure is

                                 Peruvian   invaluable   typhoid.

2. The climate of the tropics is   **anopheles   rheumatic   tropical.**

3. Specially made medicine, food, or other mixtures are

                            diseases   cinchonas   preparations.

4. Extract means   **draw out   put in   prepare.**

5. According to means **in**

                   disagreement   agreement with   a hurry.

6. A way of treating is a _____.

D-2 Bark Medicine

According to an old story, in the early seventeenth century, a Peruvian Indian was cured of a terrible fever by eating the bark of the cinchona tree. Quinine, the drug that can be extracted from cinchona bark, was not widely used as medicine until 1816.

Quinine has proved invaluable to modern medicine. It is used in the treatment of malaria, a disease transmitted by the anopheles mosquito and common in the tropical regions of the world. Quinine preparations are also used to help cure typhoid fever, rheumatic fever, and other sicknesses.

The cinchona tree belongs to the evergreen family and, unlike most evergreens, has very fragrant flowers. Cinchonas are native to

South America, but now are grown in such other places as India, Ceylon, and Java.

Although cinchona trees do not reach full size for about 8 years, the bark can be taken from 3-year-old trees. First the young trees are cut down. Next the bark is carefully stripped off, dried, and packed. It is sent to a factory where it is ground into a brown powder. From this powder, the quinine is extracted.

D-2 Testing Yourself

NUMBER RIGHT

Draw a line under each right answer or fill in each blank.

1. While not directly stated, it can be reasoned from the article that
   a. most drugs come from trees.
   b. malaria is not common throughout the United States.
   c. important discoveries are always made by scientists.

2. This article as a whole is about
   a. how medicines are discovered.   c. cinchona bark.
   b. the discovery of quinine.   d. a very valuable drug.

3. The word **It** in paragraph four refers both times to _____.

4. The cinchona tree is useful only because of its bark.

                                         Yes   No   Does not say

5. Which two sentences are not true?
   a. The cinchona is an evergreen.   c. Mosquitos carry quinine.
   b. Cinchonas reach full size in 3 years.   d. Bark may contain drugs.
                     e. Quinine helps cure malaria.

6. What word in the third paragraph means **sweet-smelling?**

Getting Ready to Read

shocking
torpedo
specimen
Mediterranean
generate
special
particular
energy
produce
stun

Draw a line under each right answer or fill in the blank.

1. **Sample** means   **special**   **specimen**   **stun**.

2. **Power** or **force** means   **shocking**   **torpedo**   **energy**.

3. **The opposite of ordinary** is

                    generate   **special**   **Mediterranean**.

4. **The opposite of general** is   **particular**   **torpedo**   **specimen**.

5. **To cause to be** means to   **stun**   **generate**   **shock**.

6. A brick falling on your head would ＿＿＿＿＿＿＿＿＿ you.

D-3   A Shocking Fish

Among the many strange fish that inhabit the waters near the bottom of the ocean, one of the most unusual is the torpedo fish. This fish, which is a member of the ray family, is flat and narrow. A large torpedo fish may measure more than a meter (about 4 feet) and may weigh from 25 to 30 kilograms (60 to 70 pounds). Yet even such a specimen will be only 8 to 10 centimeters (3 to 4 inches) thick.

These fish live mostly in warm seas. Several varieties are found in the Mediterranean Sea, in the Indian Ocean, and in the Pacific Ocean.

The torpedo fish is noted mostly for its ability to generate electricity from special organs located on both sides of its head and to give electric shocks. Getting a shock from a torpedo fish feels the same as getting a shock from a wire that carries an electrical current.

The torpedo fish uses such shocks to defend itself from enemies and to kill other fish and sea creatures for food. The strength of the shock depends on the size, strength, and energy of the particular torpedo fish. Some torpedo fish can produce a shock powerful enough to stun a person for a short time.

D-3 Testing Yourself

NUMBER RIGHT

Draw a line under each right answer or fill in each blank.

1. While not directly stated, it can be reasoned from the article that
   a. torpedo fish attack ships.   b. torpedo fish are good pets.
         c. torpedo fish can be dangerous to deep-sea divers.

2. This article as a whole is about
   a. one member of the ray family.   c. electric currents.
   b. electric fish in the ocean.   d. fishing for rays.

3. The word **one** in the first sentence refers to _____.

4. Even a large torpedo fish is rather thin.   Yes   No   Does not say

5. Which two sentences are not true?
   a. Torpedo fish may weigh 30 kilograms.
   b. Torpedo fish eat only plants.
   c. Torpedo fish usually swim near the ocean's bottom.
   d. Torpedo fish can produce electricity.
   e. The size alone of a torpedo fish determines the shock it gives.

6. What word in the third paragraph means **placed?** _____

69

Getting Ready to Read

SAY AND KNOW

costly
independently
remarkable
malleable
properties
moreover
affected
conducts
construction
utensils
appliances

Draw a line under each right answer or fill in the blank.

1. **Doing something without help from others** is **doing it**

   moreover   costly   independently.

2. It means **leads** or **escorts.**   constructs   conducts   costs

3. **Special powers** are called   **properties   appliances   utensils.**

4. **Something that can be pressed into different shapes without breaking** is called   **remarkable   malleable   affected.**

5. **Worthy of note** means   **costly   construction   remarkable.**

6. **The opposite of cheap** is _____.

D-4   Light but Strong

Not so many years ago, the metal aluminum was simply a scientific curiosity. A way of producing it was known, but this method took so much time and was so costly that very little aluminum was made or used. Then, in 1886, an American named Hall and a Frenchman named Heroult independently developed the same

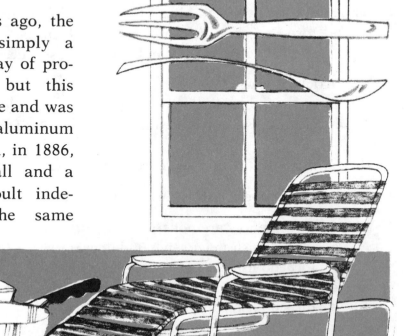

process for producing aluminum cheaply. Shortly after this, aluminum came into wide use.

Aluminum is a remarkable metal. It is malleable, which means it can be hammered into shape without breaking. Like gold and silver, aluminum hardens as it is worked. Aluminum is light in weight and, at the same time, unusually strong. These properties make it invaluable in the manufacture of airplanes. Moreover, aluminum does not rust and is not affected by salt or by salt water. It is one of our best conductors of heat and, kilogram for kilogram, it conducts electricity better than any other metal.

Because of this combination of valuable properties, aluminum is used in construction for transmitting electrical power over long distances and for making doors, windows, utensils, furniture, appliances, and many other things.

D-4 Testing Yourself   NUMBER RIGHT

Draw a line under each right answer or fill in each blank.

1. While not directly stated, it can be reasoned from the article that
     a. aluminum is hard to melt.   b. aluminum is still costly.
          c. aluminum makes very good pots and pans.

2. This article as a whole is about
     a. the discovery of aluminum.   c. making aluminum by electricity.
     b. aluminum utensils.   d. properties and uses of aluminum.

3. The word **it** in the second sentence refers to _____.

4. Aluminum is like gold and silver in one important property.
                              Yes   No   Does not say

5. Which two sentences are not true?
     a. Aluminum can be hammered without breaking.
     b. In all ways, aluminum is second to copper in conducting electricity.
     c. Aluminum is much used in construction work.
     d. Aluminum is used to make airplanes.
     e. Aluminum is not important to modern life.

6. What word in the second paragraph means **also?** _____

Getting Ready to Read

blustery
significant
events
aviation
occurred
dunes
device
derrick
convinced
available
attached

Draw a line under each right answer or fill in the blank.

1. **Things full of meaning** are   **events**   **significant**   **blustery.**

2. **Satisfied by argument** is   **occurred**   **attached**   **convinced.**

3. **Loose sand piled up by wind** makes

                                  derricks   **dunes**   **blustery.**

4. **Something that is ready for use** is said to be

                           available   **significant**   **aviation.**

5. **A derrick** is **a**   **machine**   **kind of land**   **dune.**

6. **Any mechanical thing** is called a _____.

D-5   "Blamed If They Ain't Flew!"

On a cold, blustery December day in 1903 at Kitty Hawk, North Carolina, one of the most significant events in the history of aviation occurred. On the sand dunes next to the ocean, the Wright brothers had constructed a track. On the track sat the first flying machine to have an

engine and propellers. A device consisting of a heavy weight falling from a derrick pulled the plane up the track and out into the air. The guard from the beach came running across the dunes. "They done it!" he cried. "Blamed if they ain't flew!"

Wilbur and Orville Wright were natives of Dayton, Ohio. They had operated a small bicycle shop in Dayton and had become interested in flying. After experimenting with gliders for several years, they became convinced that a power-driven machine was necessary.

At that time, there were no airplane engines available, and no one knew how to build them. The Wrights themselves built an engine, attached it to their airplane, and made their first flight. The plane stayed in the air only twelve seconds. It flew only a little over 36 meters (120 feet). But it made the most important flight in history.

D-5   Testing Yourself   NUMBER RIGHT

Draw a line under each right answer or fill in each blank.

1. While not directly stated, it can be reasoned from the article that
    a. the track made flying safer.   b. this flight was made in a glider.
        c. the track was to provide lift.

2. This article as a whole is about
    a. a great discovery.   c. the lives of two famous men.
    b. the first airplane flight.   d. the invention of engines.

3. The word **them** in the third paragraph, first sentence, refers to

_____.

4. The Wright brothers made a historic airplane flight.   Yes   No   Does not say

5. Which two sentences are not true?
    a. The Wrights built their engine.   c. The Wrights flew 36 meters.
    b. The Wrights never used gliders.   d. The Wrights used a track.
        e. No one but the Wrights saw the first plane flight.

6. What word in the first paragraph means **windy and noisy?**

_____

Getting Ready to Read

timepiece

observatory

immediately

inspected

adjusted

reset

naval

perfect

surveillance

Draw a line under each right answer or fill in the blank.

1. **Things put in balance** have been   **inspected   adjusted   reset.**

2. **Something without a flaw** is   **naval   reset   perfect.**

3. **To look at carefully** means to   **inspect   reset   naval.**

4. **A clock** is   **an observatory   a timepiece   a surveillance.**

5. **Immediately** means   **right away   soon   at a future time.**

6. **Watch kept over something** is called

_____.

D-6 Time from the Stars

How do we know that our watches and clocks are really correct? The scientist will answer, "The stars tell us."

A good watch or clock keeps time accurately. Even the best timepiece, however, must be reset occasionally if it is to maintain the correct time. We set our watches and clocks according to accurate clocks that are checked regularly with the time given by radio, television, or telephone. But where do these companies get the correct time by which they set their own clocks?

In the United States, such clocks are set according to an atomic clock kept in the Naval Observatory at Washington, DC. The world standard of time is measured from Greenwich, England, a town near

74

London. Clocks at Washington, DC, and at Greenwich, are as accurate as human skill and careful work can make them. Atomic clocks were adopted by scientists in 1958. These clocks gain or lose no more than one second in one million years!

Even the most nearly correct clocks, however, must be checked against some perfect standard. This standard is the movement of certain stars and Earth's orbit. In a sense, then, we do set our watches by the stars. The scientist's answer is correct.

D-6 Testing Yourself

NUMBER RIGHT

Draw a line under each right answer or fill in the blank.

1. While not directly stated, it can be reasoned from the article that
   a. things made by human beings are never perfect.   b. clocks are perfect.
          c. clocks must be checked against one another.

2. This article as a whole is about
   a. keeping an accurate time standard.   c. correct radio time.
   b. why scientists study the heavens.   d. telling time in the navy.

3. The word **those** in paragraph three refers to _____ .

4. Even our most exact clocks may be wrong.   Yes   No   Does not say

5. Which two sentences are not true?
   a. Time signals are given by radio.
   b. The clocks at Greenwich are checked by the position of the sun.
   c. The world standard of time is measured from Greenwich, England.
   d. All clocks must be checked at some time.
   e. The clocks at the Naval Observatory need never be checked.

6. What word in the third paragraph means **a building for watching the heavens?**

_____ .

Getting Ready to Read

SAY AND KNOW

satisfactory
fiery
volcanoes
extremely
agreeable
settlements
Scandinavians
educational
adjacent
routes

Draw a line under each right answer or fill in the blank.

1. **Ways of going** are   **volcanoes**   **routes**   **settlements.**

2. **Standing next to** means   **extremely**   **adjacent**   **fiery.**

3. **Pleasant** or **pleasing** means   **fiery**   **agreeable**   **Scandinavian.**

4. **Settlements** are   **houses**   **highways**   **colonies.**

5. **Of schooling** means   **satisfactory**   **educational**   **fiery.**

6. **The people of Norway, Sweden, and Denmark** are called

_____.

D-7   Frost and Fire

Iceland has been called the "land of frost and fire." This is a very satisfactory name, for the mountains on this island in the North Atlantic are capped with snow and ice the year around, and there are scores of fiery volcanoes.

Contrary to what most people think, however, Iceland's climate is not extremely cold. Most days are quite agreeable because of the warm current of the Gulf Stream.

When the Vikings began to settle in Iceland in A.D. 874, they found books and crosses that showed the Irish had already been there. It is likely that the Irish and Scots had come to Iceland about 70 years before the Vikings arrived. These explorers, however, had made no lasting settlements. The first real colonists were Scandinavians who came directly from Norway, Sweden, and Denmark.

The people of Iceland have very high educational standards. It was once said that more books are sold in Iceland, in relation to its population, than in any other country in the world.

Since Iceland is adjacent to one of the most important shipping routes between the United States and England, it became very important during the Second World War.

D-7 Testing Yourself

NUMBER RIGHT

Draw a line under each right answer or fill in each blank.

1. While not directly stated, it can be reasoned from the article that
    a. volcanoes make Iceland warm.   b. people read more in cold weather.
    c. some of the Irish explorers of Iceland could read.

2. This article as a whole is about
    a. the first settlers in Iceland.   c. Iceland, an interesting place.
    b. the Scandinavian countries.   d. the travels of the Vikings.

3. The word **its** in the third paragraph refers to _____.

4. The Scots established permanent settlements in Iceland.
    Yes   No   Does not say

5. Which two sentences are not true?
    a. Iceland is extremely cold.   c. Volcanoes are fiery.
    b. Iceland was important in World War II.   d. The Irish settled Iceland.
    e. The people of Iceland are great readers.

6. What word in the first paragraph means about the same as **fitting?**

Getting Ready to Read

SAY AND KNOW

separately

conditions

original

similarities

conclude

dialects

contact

numerous

isolation

Draw a line under each right answer or fill in the blank.

1. **Likenesses** means   **original   similarities   numerous.**

2. The word that means **the opposite of very few** is

     distinct   separately   numerous.

3. It means **separate.**   **dialects   distinct   conditions**

4. **Being all alone** is **being in**   **contact   isolation   condition.**

5. **The first** or **earliest one of a kind** is the

     isolation   distinct   original.

6. **To touch** means to _____.

D-8   Thousands of Languages

The speech of every group of people has developed differently. One reason for this is that each group often lived in isolation. Another reason is that each language grew up separately under different conditions. Gradually, over many centuries, some groups came in contact with other groups. When this happened, their languages grew more and more alike. In other cases, however, a group would break apart, and new languages would grow from the original one. The new languages, though distinct in many ways, would maintain similarities to one another.

There are many different countries in the world today. One might conclude that each country has its own language and that languages are only as numerous as countries. Actually, there are many more languages than there are countries. For example, in the United States, we have considered English the one language of the people. Yet at one time, on the Great Plains alone, more than 22 Native American languages were spoken.

In addition, a single language may have two or more dialects, or varieties. It is estimated that there are several thousand languages and dialects spoken in the world today.

D-8   Testing Yourself

Draw a line under each right answer or fill in each blank.

1. While not directly stated, it can be reasoned from the article that
    a. people living near one another usually have words in common.
    b. people could have learned to write earlier.
    c. people settled down too soon.

2. This article as a whole is about
    a. dialects.
    b. Native American languages.
    c. how many languages developed.
    d. the difference between language and dialect.

3. The word **one** in the first paragraph, second-to-last sentence, refers to

_____.

4. In time, some languages grew more alike.   Yes   No   Does not say

5. Which two sentences are not true?
    a. Languages are all much alike.
    b. Many Native American languages developed.
    c. There are many languages today.
    d. Dialects are varieties of a language.
    e. There are many more countries than there are languages.

6. What word in the second paragraph means **thought of carefully?**

_____

Getting Ready to Read

SAY AND KNOW

lobed

pulp

delicious

nourishing

inner

mahogany

calked

adrift

mutineers

mutiny

Draw a line under each right answer or fill in the blank.

1. Boats are **calked** to keep them from

    leaking   rotting   floating.

2. One kind of **wood** is called   calk   mahogany   lobed.

3. **Floating with no way to steer** means

    calked   adrift   mutiny.

4. **The soft part of any fruit** is called   inner   pulp   lobed.

5. **The opposite of bad-tasting** is   nourishing   lobed   delicious.

6. **People who rise up against those who are lawfully in charge** are

    called _____.

D-9   Breadfruit

The breadfruit is a rounded or oval fruit that grows on the tropical islands in the Pacific Ocean. It grows on a tree that reaches a height of about 12 meters (40 feet) and bears shiny, deeply lobed, dark green leaves, which are over 31 centimeters (1 foot) long.

The fruit is first green in color. Then it turns brown, and, if allowed to ripen fully, becomes yellow. Usually, breadfruit is gathered before it ripens and is cooked on hot stones. The pulp between the rind and the core of a breadfruit looks and feels much like new bread. When mixed with coconut milk, it makes a delicious and nourishing pudding.

The inner bark of the breadfruit tree is used to make a kind of cloth. The wood, when seasoned, looks like mahogany and is used to make furniture and to build canoes. These canoes are calked with a gum made from the sap of the tree.

Because it spoils so easily during shipping, breadfruit is not sent to northern markets.

The breadfruit tree was found in the 1770s by William Bligh, a British sea captain. Bligh later gained fame by being cast adrift by mutineers during a mutiny that took place on his ship, the *Bounty*, in 1787.

D-9 Testing Yourself

Draw a line under each right answer or fill in each blank.

1. While not directly stated, it can be reasoned from the article that
   a. breadfruit is sold in the United States.
   b. William Bligh visited tropical islands.
   c. some people make bread from breadfruit.

2. This article as a whole is about
   a. the mutiny on the *Bounty*.
   b. a British sea captain.
   c. life at sea in the 1870s.
   d. a fruit grown in the tropics.

3. The word **his** in the last sentence refers to _____ _____.

4. Breadfruit tree wood is very useful.   Yes   No   Does not say

5. Which two sentences are not true?
   a. The *Bounty* was a ship.
   b. Breadfruit is oval in shape.
   c. Breadfruit feels like bread.
   d. Canoes can be calked with breadfruit.
   e. Bligh was a mutineer on the ship *Bounty*.

6. What word in the last paragraph means **thrown** or **thrown out?**

Wings on His Feet

Laughing Eyes, a Native American princess, was loved by two young braves. One was Wasawa. Laughing Eyes liked him better. Oakana was the other. Laughing Eyes' father, the Chief, liked him better.

The Chief did not wish to force his daughter to marry Oakana. Instead, he devised a plan. He wrote two messages to a chief in the far north. Each brave was to carry one message. The first brave to return with a reply would marry Laughing Eyes. The test would be difficult, as deep snow covered the ground. Laughing Eyes was afraid that Wasawa would lose the race to Oakana, the stronger of the two.

That night, Laughing Eyes dreamed she saw ducks walking on top of the snow, while other birds sank into it. She pondered the meaning of her dream. Next morning, she scattered food for the birds. She saw that the webbing between the ducks' toes helped them to stay on top of the snow.

Laughing Eyes got a roll of soft deerskin and some pliable strips of ash. She cut thongs out of the skins, bent a strip of wood into a frame, and then fastened the ends of the wood firmly together. Next she laced the thongs back and forth from one side of the frame to the other. Before long, Laughing Eyes had fashioned two strange-looking shoes.

That evening, she recounted her dream to Wasawa. Then she showed him the shoes. She made him promise to take the shoes with him and to try them.

In a few days, the two young men set out in the snow. The sturdy Oakana soon left Wasawa far behind. When Oakana was out of sight, Wasawa put on the snowshoes. He took one step and fell. He got up, tried to walk, and fell again. He was angry, but he had promised to give the shoes a fair trial. He chose a distant tree and resolved to wear the shoes until he reached it. It took him a long while. When he arrived at his goal, he realized that he had not once sunk into the deep snow. Soon he could walk faster. Then he could run.

One day the Chief heard the call, "Wasawa is returning!" The Chief did not believe that Wasawa could have returned so quickly. He thought Wasawa was trying to deceive him. When the Chief read the answer that Wasawa had brought back, he knew Wasawa was telling the truth. He gave orders for a grand wedding feast.

Days later, Oakana arrived at the village in the north. He was told that the same message had been brought, many days before, by a brave who had wings on his feet.

Adapted from Johanna R. M. Lyback

MY READING TIME _____ (450 WORDS)

Thinking It Over

1. How was the Chief unfair to Laughing Eyes? How was he fair?

2. Can you think of another story in which a race was won by the slower runner?

3. What might have been the reasons the Chief liked Oakana better than Wasawa?

Getting Ready to Read

SAY AND KNOW

myth
character
species
brilliantly
related
domestic
introduced
adapted
especially
prairie

Draw a line under each right answer or fill in the blank.

1. **A legend** or **story** is a   **myth**   **character**   **species.**

2. **Belonging to the same family** means

                                         prairie   **adapted**   **related.**

3. **The opposite of wild** is   **introduced**   **domestic**   **brilliantly.**

4. **Particularly** means   **especially**   **brilliantly**   **prairie.**

5. **Made to fit** means   **introduced**   **related**   **adapted.**

6. **A person in a story** is called **a** _____.

E-1   One Hundred Eyes

In an ancient Greek myth, a character named Argus was said to have 100 eyes, some of which he always kept open. The name Argus has been given to a beautiful bird, known as the Argus pheasant. Although the Argus pheasant does not have 100 eyes, the male of the species does have on its wings a large number of spots that resemble eyes.

Pheasants are a group of brilliantly colored game birds that are related to chickens, turkeys, and peafowl. In western Europe and in North America, the best-known member of the pheasant family is the English pheasant. The male English pheasant usually weighs from slightly more than 1 to nearly 2 kilograms (2½ to 4 pounds), while the female weighs a little less. When living in a wild state, pheasants feed mainly on berries, roots, young plants, and insects. If pheasants are tamed, they live on the same foods as other domestic poultry.

English pheasants were successfully introduced into the United States by people interested in hunting. This bird adapted easily to the land, especially to the prairie states, and is now an important game bird in many parts of the country.

84

E-1   Testing Yourself

Draw a line under each right answer or fill in each blank.

1. While not directly stated, it can be reasoned from the article that
      a. pheasants are good to eat.   b. wild chickens eat berries.
      c. Argus pheasants have been killed off in the United States.

2. This article as a whole is about
      a. tame birds.   c. Argus pheasants.
      b. what birds eat.   d. pheasants.

3. The word **they** in the second paragraph, last sentence, refers to

                                     _____.

4. English pheasants are game birds.   Yes   No   Does not say

5. Which two sentences are not true?
      a. Pheasants can be tamed.   c. English pheasants live only in England.
      b. Pheasants live in the   d. Pheasants and turkeys are related.
      United States.
              e. The Argus pheasant is an English turkey.

6. What word in paragraph two means **brightly?** _____

Getting Ready to Read

Draw a line under each right answer or fill in the blank.

define

interferes

visibility

moisture

vapor

distribution

condenses

mixture

atmospheric

perceive

1. **To make meaning clear** is **to**

        define   interfere with   condense.

2. **To know something through your senses** is

        condenses   to perceive   a mixture.

3. **Conditions of air masses surrounding Earth** are called

        distribution   visibility   atmospheric.

4. **Wetness that can be seen in the air** is

        vapor   visibility   mixture.

5. **Slight wetness** means   **moisture   mixture   distribution.**

6. When gas changes to a liquid it _____.

E-2   Facts about Clouds

In general, we can define a cloud as anything in the atmosphere that interferes with visibility. We may perceive clouds of smoke over cities. We may perceive clouds of dust over deserts. Most people, however, when speaking of clouds, think of masses in the atmosphere that contain moisture or water vapor.

At any one time, clouds usually cover about half of the Earth's surface. Clouds are very important, for they greatly affect atmospheric movement and the distribution of the heat of the sun.

The water vapor in clouds comes from rivers, lakes, seas, and oceans. The heat of the sun continuously causes some of this water on the Earth's surface to change to vapor. This vapor, which is usually lighter than dry air, rises and combines with dust in the air to form clouds.

Some clouds contain large amounts of water vapor. When this vapor condenses into drops and falls to Earth, it is called rain. When the vapor condenses at a freezing temperature, the falling flakes are called snow. When the water vapor passes through freezing temperatures on its way to Earth, it becomes a mixture of rain and snow called sleet.

E-2   Testing Yourself

Draw a line under each right answer or fill in each blank.

1. While not directly stated, it can be reasoned from the article that
    a. not all clouds contain moisture.   b. dust clouds are red.
       c. cloudy days tend to be colder than clear days.

2. This article as a whole is about
    a. why it rains.   c. water vapor and the formation of rain.
    b. how snow forms.   d. what clouds are and how they form.

3. The word **it** in the fourth paragraph, second sentence, refers to _____.

4. All clouds contain moisture.   Yes   No   Does not say

5. Which two sentences are not true?

    a. Clouds interfere with visibility.   c. Mixed rain and sleet is snow.
    b. Rain is condensed water vapor.   d. Vapor is heavier than air.
       e. The sun's heat continuously changes water to vapor.

6. What word in the first paragraph means **large quantities together?**

Getting Ready to Read

SAY AND KNOW | Draw a line under each right answer or fill in the blank.

naturalists

spines

seldom

bordering

continents

excretes

coaxes

birth

female

biologists

1. It is **the opposite of often.**   seldom   bordering   spines

2. **Located at the edge of** means   birth   naturalists   bordering.

3. **Persons skilled in the science of life** are
continents   females   biologists.

4. **Stiff, sharp things like thorns** are called
spines   females   naturalists.

5. It means **gets rid of.**   coaxes   excretes   continents

6. **Coming into life** or **being born** is called _____.

E-3   A Watery Nest

Biologists and other natural-ists have discovered that there are several kinds of fish that build real nests under the water. Perhaps the most interesting of these nest-building fish is one called the stickleback, which gets its name from the sharp spines that grow on its back.

Approximately a dozen different kinds of sticklebacks have been found. Among these are both fresh and saltwater varieties. All sticklebacks are rather small fish that are seldom more than 15 centimeters (6 inches) long. Freshwater sticklebacks are found in the ponds, small lakes, and streams of North America, Europe, and Asia and in the oceans bordering these continents.

In spring, the male stickleback builds his nest on the bottom of the body of water in which he lives.

This nest is constructed of such things as sticks, leaves, bits of straw, and sand, which he glues together with a special liquid that he excretes.

When he finishes building his nest, the male stickleback coaxes the female to enter it and lay her eggs. Then the female leaves, never to return. The male guards his nest until the eggs are hatched and watches over the young fish for several days after their birth.

E-3 Testing Yourself

NUMBER RIGHT

Draw a line under each right answer or fill in each blank.

1. While not directly stated, it can be reasoned from the article that
    a. sticklebacks live in the tropics.   b. most fish do not build nests.
        c. it is difficult for sticklebacks to live in sea water.

2. This article as a whole is about
    a. nest-building animals.   c. the stickleback and its nest.
    b. a kind of fish.   d. freshwater fish and their nests.

3. The word **it** in the fourth paragraph refers to _____.

4. The female stickleback guards her young well.   Yes   No   Does not say

5. Which two sentences are not true?
    a. The male stickleback builds the nest.
    b. Sticklebacks are seldom less than 15 centimeters long.
    c. The stickleback builds his nest near the top of the water.
    d. Sticklebacks are found in fresh water.
    e. Sticklebacks are found in North America.

6. What word in the third paragraph means **built?** _____

Getting Ready to Read

strength
cubic
flares
surface
peculiarly
flammable
exposed
durable
durability
magnesium
aluminum

Draw a line under each right answer or fill in the blank.

1. To use force you need   **durability   strength   magnesium.**

2. **Anything that will last for a long time** is
   durable   flammable   aluminum.

3. **Something that can be set on fire easily** is called
   flammable   exposed   surface.

4. **In a strange manner** means   **flammable   peculiarly   flares.**

5. A form shaped like a cube is   **exposed   surface   cubic.**

6. **The outside** of anything is **the** _____.

E-4   Metal from the Ocean

Magnesium is one of the strongest and most wonderful of all metals. It is peculiarly light and, when properly combined with other metals, very strong and durable. Lightness, durability, and strength

are valuable qualities in any substance, but they are qualities most valuable of all in a metal. A cubic meter of steel weighs 7922 kilograms (17,410 pounds). A cubic meter of aluminum, which is one of the lightest of metals, weighs 2812 kilograms (6180 pounds). A cubic meter of magnesium, however, weighs only 1800 kilograms (3955 pounds). When combined with other metals, magnesium is very useful in the making of airplanes. It is also used to protect underground oil and gas lines.

Magnesium in powdered form is highly flammable when exposed to air. In fact, it burns nearly as quickly as gasoline and is used for signal flares.

90

Magnesium is found in many different places on the Earth's surface. However, it is always found in combination with other substances. Magnesium is also found in sea water. It is a long, hard task to separate magnesium from salt water. In spite of this fact, ways of doing it have been invented, and much of the present magnesium supply comes from the sea.

E-4 Testing Yourself

NUMBER RIGHT

Draw a line under each right answer or fill in each blank.

1. While not directly stated, it can be reasoned from the article that
    a. heavy metals are stronger than light ones.
    b. magnesium would be better than steel for eyeglass frames.
    c. magnesium is now found only in sea water.

2. This article as a whole is about
    a. taking magnesium from the sea.
    b. making airplanes of aluminum.
    c. magnesium.
    d. durable metals.

3. The word **it** in the third paragraph, second sentence, refers to

_____.

4. Magnesium is stronger than aluminum.   Yes   No   Does not say

5. Which two sentences are not true?
    a. Powdered magnesium burns easily.
    b. Magnesium must be used alone.
    c. Magnesium is found in salt water.
    d. Light, weak metal is most useful.
    e. Steel weighs much more than aluminum.

6. What word in paragraph one means **in the correct way?**

_____

Getting Ready to Read

SAY AND KNOW

contribute

comfort

convenience

immeasurably

alpacas

bred

quantities

extensively

predominates

mature

Draw a line under each right answer or fill in the blank.

1. **Saving of trouble** means   **bred**   **convenience**   **alpacas.**

2. It means **has the top position.**

               contributes   **matures**   **predominates**

3. **Full-grown** means   **bred**   **immeasurably**   **mature.**

4. **The opposite of take** is   **comfort**   **contribute**   **extensively.**

5. **Amounts** are   **extensively**   **convenience**   **quantities.**

6. **South American animals with long, silky wool** are called

_____.

E-5   Wool Producers

Various kinds of domestic animals, such as horses and cows, contribute immeasurably to our comfort and convenience. Sheep hold a primary place among these animals. Wool, which is the warm, soft, hairy covering of some animals, may be obtained from llamas, alpacas, and goats as well as from sheep. In spite of this, almost all of our useful wool crop comes from the sheep.

Although there are a number of different kinds of wool-producing sheep, merino sheep are the most extensively known wool-producing animals in the world. Originally bred in Spain, these sheep are now at home in many parts of the world. Along with all the other types of wool-producing sheep, merinos are raised in the United States.

At shearing time, the wool is clipped from the sheep. It is then washed, cleaned, and made into thread. A half kilogram (slightly more than a pound) of fine wool will make about 160 kilometers (about 100 miles) of thread, and one mature merino ram may yield as much as 12 kilograms (28 pounds) of wool at a single shearing.

Such countries as the United States, Great Britain, Russia, and Argentina send large quantities of wool to market. Australia, how-ever, predominates in wool production.

E-5 Testing Yourself

Draw a line under each right answer or fill in each blank.

1. While not directly stated, it can be reasoned from the article that
   a. merino sheep grow well in most countries.
   b. Australia has fewer sheep than the United States.
   c. merino sheep came first from South America.

2. This article as a whole is about
   a. wool from merino llamas.
   b. making wool cloth.
   c. wool and wool-producing animals.
   d. human comfort and convenience.

3. The word **it** in the third paragraph, second sentence, refers to _____.

4. Merino sheep are produced only for wool.   Yes   No   Does not say

5. Which two sentences are not true?
   a. Russia produces much wool.
   b. Merinos are found in the U.S.
   c. Merinos are raised only in Spain.
   d. Wool comes only from sheep.
   e. Wool is made into thread before it is used.

6. What word in the second paragraph means **at first?** _____

Getting Ready to Read

SAY AND KNOW

astronomers

sample

random

questionnaire

telescope

binoculars

recommend

section

result

Draw a line under each right answer or fill in the blank.

1. You look through them to see faraway things.

                                               sample   **binoculars**   **random**

2. It means **by chance.**   result   random   recommend

3. A part of something is **a**   questionnaire   section   telescope.

4. It **has many questions.**   telescope   questionnaire   binoculars

5. They study the stars.   result   sample   astronomers

6. When you say that **something is good,** you _____it.

E-6 How Many Stars?

If you count all the stars you can see, you will reach almost 3000. If you use binoculars, the number will be about 50,000. If you use a large telescope, there will be about 500,000,000. But to count that high,

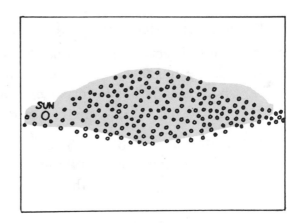

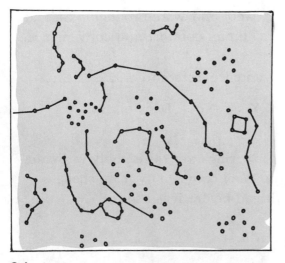

you will have to spend every night of your whole life counting.

Do astronomers really know how many stars there are? They do not count them all. They take samples. They divide the sky into many small sections. Then they count the stars in some sections in different parts of the sky. From these numbers, they figure out about how many stars there are in the whole sky.

This system works only if the samples are good. First of all, the samples must be large enough. An advertisement says that four out of five dentists recommend a certain toothbrush. Will you believe the ad if you learn that only five dentists, out of the hundreds of thousands in the country, had been asked?

Samples also must be random. This means they must be chosen completely by chance. A town's mayor who wanted to find out what the people thought might send out a questionnaire. But if the questionnaire went only to friends, would you think the results would reflect the opinions of the whole town?

E-6 Testing Yourself

NUMBER RIGHT

Draw a line under each right answer or fill in each blank.

1. While not directly stated, it can be reasoned from the article that
    a. you cannot trust any samples.
    b. samples that are too small may give wrong answers.
    c. toothbrush advertisements are false.

2. This article as a whole is about
    a. the use of samples.   c. dentists.
    b. millions of stars.   d. questionnaires.

3. The word **they** in the last paragraph, second sentence, refers to

    _____.

4. Many things are too large to be counted.   Yes   No   Does not say

5. Which two sentences are not true?
    a. Astronomers know exactly how many stars there are.
    b. You can see more stars through a telescope than with binoculars.
    c. Samples should be chosen on the basis of chance.
    d. If you have good eyes, you can see over 2000 stars on a clear night.
    e. One section of the sky is good enough as a sample.

6. What word in the last paragraph means **picked out?** _____

Getting Ready to Read

Draw a line under each right answer or fill in the blank.

collide

control

violent

suitable

armadillo

penguin

establish

preserves

difficult

1. It is **an animal with armor for protection.**

                                               penguin   armadillo   control

2. It means **to bump into someone.**   suitable   collide   violent

3. It means about the same as **to build.**

                                      establish   preserves   difficult

4. It means **with great force.**   control   difficult   violent

5. It means **fit** or **appropriate.**   suitable   collide   preserves

6. Parks built to protect animals are sometimes called _____.

E-7   It Will Blow Past You

"If you want to see Patagonia, just sit still. It will all blow past you." So it is said about the southern tip of South America. The violent winds of Patagonia are called *pamperos*. Birds have been seen to lose control in such winds and collide with each other.

Patagonia belongs partly to Chile, partly to Argentina. Argentine Patagonia, on the east, is a dry, flat land on which little grows except a few bushes. Chile's part of Patagonia, on the west, has heavily wooded strips. This area gets more

96

rain than the Argentine section, and it includes part of the Andes Mountains.

The land is suitable for raising cattle and sheep. There is also coal, oil, and timber, but it has been difficult to get these products to market.

Of greatest interest are the unusual animals. Rheas, which look like ostriches, and guanacos, cousins of the camel, are found in eastern Patagonia. Here the armadillo has lived unchanged for 45 million years. Whales, sea lions, and dolphins live in the sea nearby. And penguins crowd the beaches by the millions.

At one time, these animals were nearly wiped out by hunters. Now wildlife preserves are being established to protect the animals. The rich animal life of Patagonia is returning to normal.

E-7 Testing Yourself

NUMBER RIGHT

Draw a line under each right answer or fill in each blank.

1. While not directly stated, it can be reasoned from the article that
    a. only animals live in Patagonia.
    b. Patagonia is not a nation like Chile and Argentina.
    c. few birds are able to live in Patagonia because of the fierce wind.

2. This article as a whole is about
    a. animals of Patagonia.   c. the tip of South America.
    b. pamperos.   d. Argentina and Chile.

3. The word **it** in the second sentence refers to _____.

4. Some animals in Patagonia are the same way today as they were millions of years ago.   Yes   No   Does not say

5. Which two sentences are not true?
    a. Pamperos are Patagonian fish.
    b. Patagonia is the southern tip of North America.
    c. Two nations own Patagonia.
    d. Ostriches and rheas look alike.
    e. Guanacos are found in Argentine Patagonia.

6. What word in the third paragraph means **not easy?** _____

Getting Ready to Read

SAY AND KNOW

improvement
represented
direction
signify
organize
logical
increasingly
symbols
curve
crossbones
favorable
circumstances

Draw a line under each right answer or fill in the blank.

1. **Less and less** is **opposite to**   increasingly   direction   logical.

2. **All signs** are   **symbols**   **curves**   **crossbones**.

3. **Something getting better** shows

logical   favorable   improvement.

4. **Conditions** are   **circumstances**   **crossbones**   **organize**.

5. **An idea that is sensible** or **reasonable** is

favorable   logical   represented.

6. **To be a sign of** means **to** _____.

E-8   Idea Signs

Picture writing was probably originated by people who lived centuries ago in a time that is called the Stone Age. It has also been employed by many people since then. Some Native Americans, for example, were still using this method of communicating when this country was being settled.

As people grew more civilized, some of them were able to develop increasingly better ways of written communication than simple picture writing. In about the year 3000 B.C., the Egyptians, a people living under favorable circumstances in the Nile Valley of northern Africa,

took the next step in the improvement of written language. They developed a written language in which written symbols represented ideas. Such idea signs are called *hieroglyphics*.

Even today we still use symbols. One is a figure "S" that warns of a double curve; another is an arrow to point out the right direction; and a third is a skull and crossbones to signify poison.

After idea signs, the Egyptians used pictures of sounds people made in saying words. The next logical step, which the ancient Egyptians never took, would have been to organize these signs into an alphabet of letters.

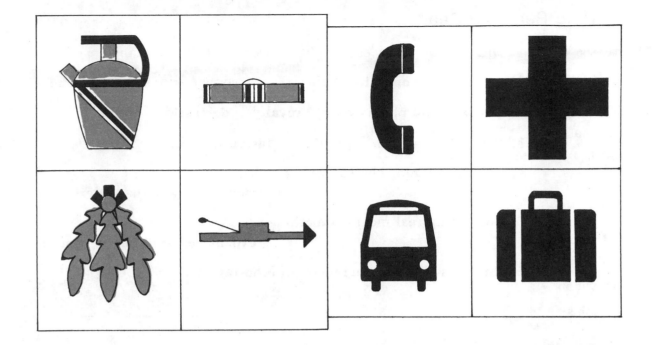

E-8 Testing Yourself

Draw a line under each right answer or fill in each blank.

1. While not directly stated, it can be reasoned from the article that
   - a. favorable circumstances help people to develop.
   - b. Native Americans were the first to use picture writing.
   - c. some picture writing is still used to represent ideas.

2. This article as a whole is about
   - a. early written language.
   - b. writing of Native Americans.
   - c. the Stone Age writing.
   - d. the Nile Valley.

3. The word **it** in sentence two refers to _____ _____.

4. Early Egyptians used letters in their writing.   Yes   No   Does not say

5. Which two sentences are not true?
   - a. Egyptians lived in Africa
   - b. Egyptians invented an alphabet.
   - c. Hieroglyphics are idea signs.
   - d. We do not use symbols today.
   - e. The Egyptians developed hieroglyphics.

6. What word in paragraph two means **stood for?** _____

99

Getting Ready to Read

expensive

genuine

political

social

role

appropriate

royalty

instance

derivation

ransoms

Draw a line under each right answer or fill in the blank.

1. It means **the opposite of cheap.**   ransoms   expensive   social

2. **The part you play** is **your**   royalty   derivation   role.

3. It means **example.**   political   instance   role

4. **What something comes from** is called **its**
                                appropriate   genuine   derivation.

5. **Something real** means **something**
                                expensive   political   genuine.

6. **Amounts paid for the release of a hostage** are

_____.

E-9   A Royal Present

Pepper is one of the earliest spices known. It has probably played the most important political and social role of any spice. At one time, pepper was so expensive that ½ kilogram (slightly more than a pound) of it was considered an appropriate present for royalty to give or receive. In early times, taxes were often paid with pepper. There are genuine historical records telling how ransoms were partly paid with quantities of pepper.

Pepper is obtained from a plant that climbs a tree as ivy does. When the plants are cultivated,

poles are set up on which the vines can climb. The pepper plant begins to bear in 4 or 5 years and will produce heavily for 14 or 15 years. It is a native of the warm islands of the East Indies and is now grown in many tropical countries.

The small, green berries of the pepper plants are harvested before they are ripe. As they dry in the sunshine or over a slow fire, they turn black. After they are reduced to a powder, they become what we call black pepper. The derivation of white pepper is the same. In this instance, the berries of the plants have been allowed to ripen before being ground.

E-9 Testing Yourself

NUMBER RIGHT

Draw a line under each right answer or fill in each blank.

1. While not directly stated, it can be reasoned from the article that
   a. pepper plants can be grown in the United States.
   b. pepper plants need hot weather to grow.
   c. pepper plants may live to be 30 years old.

2. This article as a whole is about
   a. making black pepper.   c. cultivating pepper plants.
   b. an important spice.   d. the importance of growing pepper.

3. The word **it** in the second paragraph, last sentence, refers to

   _____ _____.

4. Pepper was once expensive.   Yes   No   Does not say

5. Which two sentences are not true?
   a. Pepper was once valuable.   c. Black pepper is made with ripe berries.
   b. Pepper is a climbing plant. d. Pepper first was used 25 years ago.
              e. Once people often paid taxes with pepper.

6. What word in the first paragraph means **fitting** or **just right**?

   _____

How Buck Saved His Master

John Thornton and his partners, Hans and Pete, were taking a boat down a bad stretch of rapids in the wilderness. The partners moved along the bank, guiding the boat with ropes. Thornton himself stood in the boat, helping with a pole. Buck, Thornton's dog, ran along the bank, keeping abreast of the boat. His eyes never left Thornton.

At one especially bad spot, Hans loosened the rope, and Thornton poled the boat into midstream to clear a submerged ledge. The hazard was successfully passed, but Hans checked the rope too quickly as the boat flew downstream. Over it went, and Thornton was swept toward the wild water below, where no swimmer could live.

Buck sprang into the river. After a hard swim, he caught up with Thornton. When he felt his master grasp his tail, the big dog headed for the bank. Buck was a powerful swimmer, but he, too, was carried rapidly downstream. Thornton saw that it was impossible for them to reach shore. Smashing into a rock with crushing force, he desperately clutched its slippery top with both hands. Above the roar of the churning water, he shouted, "Go, Buck, go!"

Buck obediently struggled shoreward and was pulled out by Peter and Hans. The men knew that Thornton could not cling to the slippery rock for long. They ran up the bank to a point above Thornton. Tying a rope about Buck's neck and shoulders, they put him once more into the water.

Buck struck out boldly, but the rushing water carried him helplessly past Thornton.

Hans hauled back on the rope, jerking Buck under the water as he pulled the big dog ashore. Buck was half drowned, and Hans and Pete had to pound breath back into him. The faint sound of Thornton's calls, however, acted upon Buck. He sprang to his feet and threw himself into the stream once again. This time he swam straight toward a spot above his master. When he was directly above Thornton, Buck hurtled downstream toward him.

Buck struck Thornton like a battering ram. The man threw his arms around Buck's shaggy neck. Hans wound the rope about a tree on the bank. He and Pete pulled with all their might.

Buck and Thornton were jerked under the water. Strangling, choking, smashing against rocks and snags, they were slowly pulled to shore.

When Thornton finally came to, his first thought was for Buck, who lay nearby. Although bruised and battered himself, Thornton carefully checked Buck's body. To his relief, he found only three broken ribs.

"That settles it," he announced, "we camp right here." And camp they did until Buck was able to travel again.

Adapted from Jack London

MY READING TIME _____ (450 WORDS)

Thinking It Over

1. What incidents in the story help you to understand how devoted Buck and Thornton were to one another?

2. What did Buck learn about the river the first two times he tried to save Thornton? How did he apply what he had learned?

3. If Buck had not been along, how might Hans and Pete have saved Thornton?

Getting Ready to Read

human
speech
facility
phrases
varieties
proficient
starling
varying
appealing
popularity
aptitude
mimicking

Draw a line under each right answer or fill in the blank.

1. **Special ability** means   **aptitude**   **popularity**   **starling.**

2. It means **imitating.**   **phrases**   **mimicking**   **varying**

3. Another word for **talk** is   **varieties**   **speech**   **mimicking.**

4. **Skilled** means   **appealing**   **facility**   **proficient.**

5. **Popularity** is **the state of being liked by**
           most people   **no one**   **a few people.**

6. **Without difficulty** means **with** _____.

F-1   Talking Birds

The parrot is able to imitate human speech more effectively than any other bird. Many parrots have great facility in imitating not only human speech but also other human sounds. They may be taught to

speak words, phrases, and sometimes whole sentences. They also have aptitude for learning to whistle, laugh, cry, and sing.

The parrot family is a large one, having several hundred varieties. These are native to such warm parts of the world as the tropics of Asia, Africa, Australia, and South America. Parrots are usually brilliantly colored. They vary in size from 1 meter to only 8 centimeters (about 3 inches) long.

Another bird sometimes very proficient at mimicking human speech is a member of the starling family, the myna bird, which is common to India, Burma, and other

parts of Asia. Myna birds are richly colored, varying from dark reddish-brown to black, with white-tipped wings and bright yellow legs and bills.

Both parrots and myna birds may be kept in cages as house pets. Their ability to imitate human sounds makes them very appealing. Parakeets, a small variety of parrot, have been popular pets for decades.

F-1   Testing Yourself

NUMBER RIGHT

Draw a line under each right answer or fill in each blank.

1. While not directly stated, it can be reasoned from the article that
   a. birds are the only animals that can imitate speech.
   b. parrots have sweet voices.
   c. in France, a parrot would speak in French.

2. This article as a whole is about
   a. birds that can imitate speech.   c. parakeets as pets.
   b. myna birds and their coloring.   d. birds for pets.

3. The word **these** in the second paragraph, second sentence, refers to

   _____.

4. Macaws can be taught to talk.   Yes   No   Does not say

5. Which two sentences are not true?
   a. Parakeets are small parrots.   c. Myna birds come from Asia.
   b. Mynas are small parrots.   d. Few parrots can learn to speak.
          e. Parrots vary greatly in size.

6. What word in the third paragraph means **copying closely?**

   _____

Getting Ready to Read

illuminate
mineral
utilized
agriculture
violently
sufficient
ignites
friction
congregate
vital

Draw a line under each right answer or fill in the blank.

1. **To light up** means **to   utilize   illuminate   congregate.**

2. If it is **sufficient**, it is   **enough   too much   not enough.**

3. Having **made use of** means   **mineral   illuminated   utilized.**

4. If you strike a match properly, it
   frictions   congregates   ignites.

5. **The opposite of gently** is   **vital   violently   sufficiently.**

6. **Farming** may also be called _____.

F-2   Nature's Lights

When you see a firefly flitting through the air on a dark summer night, you may wonder at the source of its light. This light comes from a mineral called phosphorus, which is found in small amounts in the body of the firefly. Phosphorus is also found in the bodies of many kinds of deep-sea fish. Sometimes, when large numbers of these fish congregate near the surface of the ocean, their bodies illuminate an area that can be seen for long distances.

Phosphorus is also found in many parts of our bodies and is essential to human life. In modern times, many vital uses have been found for this mineral. Large amounts of phosphorus are utilized in medicines, in agriculture, and in manufacturing.

Perhaps the most generally familiar place to find phosphorus is in the heads of matches. Because phosphorus burns violently at low temperatures, the small amount of heat produced by the friction of rubbing the head of a match against a rough surface is sufficient to cause the phosphorus in the match head to burn. As the head of the match ignites, it lights the wood or paper that forms the body of the match.

F-2 Testing Yourself   NUMBER RIGHT

Draw a line under each right answer or fill in each blank.

1. While not directly stated, it can be reasoned from the article that
    a. phosphorus was not widely used among the ancients.
    b. phosphorus is found in the bodies of many animals.
    c. phosphorus is a mineral not widely used.

2. This article as a whole is about
    a. making matches.   c. fireflies and fish.
    b. the mineral phosphorus.   d. minerals.

3. The word **it** in the last sentence refers to _____.

4. Matches contain phosphorus.   Yes   No   Does not say

5. Which two sentences are not true?
    a. Phosphorus ignites at low temperatures.
    b. Phosphorus is found in the human body.
    c. Phosphorus is used in agriculture.
    d. Fireflies are the only animals that produce light because of phosphorus.
    e. Phosphorus is used only in agriculture.

6. What word in the second paragraph, first sentence, means **most important?**

Getting Ready to Read

prey
cylindrical
cling
piers
wharves
stationary
located
surrounded
ejects
irritates

Draw a line under each right answer or fill in the blank.

1. **Victim** means   **prey**   **piers**   **wharves.**

2. **To hang on** means **to**   **locate**   **cling**   **eject.**

3. A car **standing still** is   **surrounded**   **cylindrical**   **stationary.**

4. **A roller-shaped object** is   **cylindrical**   **wharves**   **stationary.**

5. **Throws out** means   **irritates**   **located**   **ejects.**

6. An action that stirs up anger _____.

F-3   Undersea Cowhands

We all know how a cowhand ropes a calf. An underwater animal called the sea anemone lassos its prey in much the same manner.

Most sea anemones are cylindrical in shape and are as broad as they are high. They cling to the bottom of the sea, to seaweed at the ocean's surface, to rocks, and to the wooden piers of wharves and bridges. Sea anemones are almost stationary, and can move only very slowly over the surfaces to which they are attached. Few sea anemones measure more than 8 centimeters (about 3 inches) across.

The sea anemone's mouth is located at its top. The mouth is surrounded by one or more circles of tentacles, or long arms. In each tentacle is a special kind of cell. When anything irritates the tentacle, this cell ejects a pointed thread that carries poison. Any small fish or animal struck by this poisoned thread becomes helpless, just as a calf caught by a cowhand's rope is helpless.

Sea anemones are beautifully colored. They get their name because they resemble anemones, or wind flowers, which are plants with many-colored flowers that bloom in spring.

F-3 Testing Yourself

Draw a line under each right answer or fill in each blank.

1. While not directly stated, it can be reasoned from the article that

    a. sea anemones can swim.   b. sea anemones look like snails.

    c. small sea animals are not safe around sea anemones.

2. This article as a whole is about

    a. a dangerous plant.   c. a lasso plant.

    b. plants that look like animals.   d. an animal that resembles a flower.

3. The word **its** in the third paragraph, first sentence, refers to

_____.

4. Sea anemones carry poison in special cells.   Yes   No   Does not say

5. Which two sentences are not true?

    a. Sea anemones move about rapidly.   c. Anemones are wild flowers.

    b. Sea anemones eat mostly plants.   d. Sea anemones have tentacles.

    e. In each tentacle is a special cell.

6. What word in the third paragraph means **shoots out?** _____

Getting Ready to Read

Draw a line under each right answer or fill in the blank.

1. Something not pleasant to look at is

solution   unsightly   preferred.

2. A process of getting rid of something is

disposal   recycling   waste.

3. Brought into being is _____ .

4. The **answer to something** is its _____ .

5. The process of burning to ashes is known as

recycling   incineration   disposal.

6. Two words that mean **useless, discarded material** are

_____ , _____ .

F-4   Garbage Is Big Business

What happens to the garbage and trash in your house? In the United States it is estimated that each person produces about 2,000 pounds (about 900 kilograms) of waste every year. Our increasing production of waste materials has given modern society tough problems to solve. But the solutions to these problems have also created new industries and jobs.

Waste disposal is what happens to your garbage and trash. There are three ways to dispose of solid waste: landfills, incineration, and recycling.

This is a picture of a landfill.

You can see that it is unsightly, unhealthy, and dangerous. Many landfills today do not look like this,

110

however. In a safe landfill, the waste is first cleaned up and shredded, then covered with earth.

Incineration, or burning at very high temperatures, can reduce waste to steam. The steam is then often used as fuel by industry. The largest incineration plant in the United States is in Chicago, Illinois.

Recycling is a good method of waste disposal, for many reasons. To recycle means to use again. The recycling of waste metals, for example, is an important conservation practice. People now work in recycling centers where metal, glass, paper, and plastic are recycled for reuse. New industries are also finding ways to reduce solid waste by cutting down on paper packaging.

Finally, scientists are creating new substances that are easier to recycle. Garbage has become big business!

F-4   Testing Yourself   **NUMBER RIGHT**

Draw a line under each right answer or fill in the blank.

1. While not directly stated, it can be reasoned from the article that
    a. people can make money in the garbage business.
    b. one way to dispose of waste is by incineration.
    c. gases released by burning can be harmful.

2. This article as a whole is about
    a. ways that plastics are recycled.
    b. a new industry.
    c. how landfills are constructed.
    d. paper waste in fast-food stores.

3. There is no way to dispose of solid waste.   Yes   No   Does not say

4. To **recycle** means to use again.   Yes   No   Does not say

5. Which two sentences are not true?
    a. There are three ways to dispose of solid waste.
    b. There are no safe landfills.
    c. Paper and glass can be recycled.
    d. Recycling has created jobs and industries.
    e. People enjoy living near landfills.

6. What word in the third paragraph means **unsafe**? _____

Getting Ready to Read

SAY AND KNOW

conceived
emergencies
acrobats
nylon
release
pilot
chute
automatically
canopy
unharmed

Draw a line under each right answer or fill in the blank.

1. **The short form of parachute** is   chute   pilot   nylon.

2. It is **a cover.**   automatically   canopy   release

3. It means **thought of.**   canopy   pilot   conceived

4. **People who perform stunts** are   acrobats   chutes   emergencies.

5. **The opposite of hurt** is   conceived   unharmed   release.

6. A fiber which is made in a factory is _____.

F-5   Escape Through the Air

Early airplane pilots had no parachutes. It soon became clear that some scheme had to be conceived that would allow people to escape from planes in emergencies.

Chinese acrobats are believed to have used parachutelike devices in the year 1306. Leonardo da Vinci thought of the basic idea

for parachutes in 1495. In 1797, Garnerin of France made the first real parachute jump from a balloon. He landed safely. Through the years, many other experiments were made. Finally, the modern parachute was developed. Today people do parachute jumping for sport as well as to save lives.

Most modern parachutes are made of nylon. They measure about 9 meters (28 feet) across. A modern parachute can be folded into a package that weighs less than 8 kilograms (18 pounds). When it becomes necessary to leave a plane in flight, a person puts on a parachute, jumps out of the plane, and pulls the release cord. A small pilot

parachute opens first. This pilot chute then pulls the main chute open.

Some parachutes today are made to open automatically. When the parachute spreads into a canopy above the falling person, the speed of fall is reduced to about 22 kilometers (about 14 miles) an hour. Chances of reaching the earth unharmed are good.

F-5 Testing Yourself

NUMBER RIGHT

Draw a line under each right answer or fill in each blank.

1. While not directly stated, it can be reasoned from the article that
   - a. the Chinese are more daring than other people.
   - b. plane passengers all wear parachutes.
   - c. some people enjoy dangerous sports.

2. This article as a whole is about
   - a. airplane travel.
   - b. the modern parachute.
   - c. the people who helped invent the parachute.
   - d. the origin and improvement of parachutes.

3. The word **they** in the third paragraph, second sentence, refers to

   _____.

4. A parachute breaks the speed of a falling body.   Yes   No   Does not say

5. Which two sentences are not true?
   - a. All parachutes open by themselves.
   - b. All modern parachutes are of silk.
   - c. Parachutes today are light in weight.
   - d. Parachutes are safety devices.
   - e. The first parachute jump from a balloon was made in 1797.

6. What word in the last paragraph means **made smaller or less?**

   _____

Getting Ready to Read

SAY AND KNOW

zero

molecule

example

extremely

kilometer

mathematics

distance

billion

trillion

Draw a line under each right answer or fill in the blank.

1. **It is 1000 meters.**   kilometer   molecule   zero

2. **The study of numbers and shapes** is

   kilometer   trillion   mathematics.

3. **It means especially** or **very.**   distance   zero   extremely

4. **The figure 0 is a**   zero   distance   billion.

5. **A molecule is very**   tall   large   small.

6. **For instance** means about the same as **for** _____.

F-6   Think Big!

If you were asked to give a name to the largest number you could think of, what would it be? A child who was asked this question once thought of the name *googol.* Now *googol* is used in mathematics to mean the number 1 followed by 100 zeros.

A googol is much, much larger than a million. But can you think how large a million is? Suppose you start counting. You count at the rate of one number each second. You will reach a million 12 full days from now, and there will have been no time for you to eat or sleep.

Will you be able to live for a million days? If so, you will be nearly 2740 years old!

Do we really need such large numbers? Yes, if we try to understand our world. Molecules of water, for example, are extremely small. Suppose you pour a million of them each second into a quart jar. It would take you well over a million years to fill that jar.

The stars in the Milky Way number over 100 billion. These stars are so far away we use "light years" (about 9400 trillion kilometers, or about 5837 trillion miles) to measure their distance. Our nearest star after the sun is about 37 trillion kilometers (about 23 trillion miles) away.

F-6   Testing Yourself

NUMBER RIGHT

Draw a line under each right answer or fill in each blank.

1. While not directly stated, it can be reasoned from the article that
   a. no one number is the "largest possible number."
   b. molecules are so small that they do not weigh anything.
   c. nobody can count to a million.

2. This article as a whole is about
   a. large numbers.   c. molecules of water.
   b. googols.   d. light years.

3. The word **it** in the first sentence refers to

   _____ _____.

4. There are fewer than 100 billion stars in the Milky Way.

                          Yes   No   Does not say

5. Which two sentences are not true?
   a. A child made up the name *googol*.
   b. A googol is not a real number.
   c. Water molecules are very small.
   d. A million is larger than a googol.
   e. Probably no one has ever lived for a million days.

6. What word in the second paragraph, fourth sentence, means about the same as

   speed? _____

Getting Ready to Read

SAY AND KNOW

disbanded

preserving

creating

nestled

physical

tropical

exist

volcanoes

democratic

Spaniards

Draw a line under each right answer or fill in the blank.

1. **People from Spain** are called _____.

2. **A self-governing nation** is _____.

3. To **lie sheltered or partly hidden** is

                    tropical   disbanded   nestled.

4. **A place that is very hot** is   **democratic   nestled   tropical.**

5. **An organization that has been broken up** has been

                               _____.

6. Which word means **making?**   **existing   creating   preserving**

F-7   The Rich Coast

What would you think of a country where 93 percent of the people can read and write? Where the army has been disbanded? Where preserving the beauty of the land is so important to the people that the country is a leader in creating national parks? If all this sounds good to you, visit Costa Rica.

Nestled between Nicaragua and Panama in Central America, Costa Rica has great physical beauty. Mountains, sandy beaches, tropical rain forests, and active volcanoes all exist in this small democratic country.

116

About half of Costa Rica's 3½ million people live in big cities like the capital, San Jose. The other half live in the countryside, and grow bananas, coffee, corn, and rice.

Costa Ricans are right to be proud of their strong educational goals, their democratic government, and their close families.

When the Spaniards came to this land in the early 1500's they named it Costa Rica, which means rich coast. When the Spaniards said "rich," they were hoping for gold (which they never found). But Costa Rica has proved to be rich in other, more important, ways.

F-7   Testing Yourself   **NUMBER RIGHT**

Draw a line under each right answer or fill in each blank.

1. While not directly stated, it can be reasoned from the article that
   a. the Costa Ricans are a happy people.
   b. the people of Costa Rica are much like the people of Canada.
   c. Costa Rica does a lot of business in manufacturing.

2. This article as a whole is about
   a. bananas.
   b. life on a coffee plantation.
   c. the many rulers of Costa Rica.
   d. a country in Central America.

3. The word **they** in the last paragraph, first sentence refers to

   _____.

4. Three and a half million people live in Costa Rica.   Yes   No   Does not say

5. Which two sentences are not true?
   a. Most of the people of Costa Rica can read and write.
   b. Costa Rica's capital is San Jose.
   c. Costa Ricans are proud of their army and navy.
   d. Costa Rica was discovered by French explorers.
   e. About half of the people of Costa Rica live in cities.

6. Which word in the first paragraph means **the first or foremost**?

   _____

Getting Ready to Read

Japanese
Chinese
formerly
major
carving
initiated
refined
preferred
syllable
alphabet
alphabetically
hieroglyphic

Draw a line under each right answer or fill in the blank.

1. **Improved** means   **refined**   **preferred**   **initiated.**

2. **The opposite of minor** is   **formerly**   **alphabetically**   **major.**

3. The **cutting** of designs in jade is   **Chinese**   **carving**   **syllable.**

4. **Something begun** has been   **refined**   **formerly**   **initiated.**

5. It means **liked better.**   **alphabet**   **preferred**   **Japanese**

6. It is a word or a part of a word that is said as a unit.

_____

F-8   Writing without an Alphabet

We think of written language in terms of words composed of the letters of an alphabet. However,

linguists tell us that alphabets are relatively modern and that people were able to communicate by writing for a long time before any group invented an alphabet.

One early kind of written language was in the form of picture writing called *hieroglyphics*. The ancient Egyptians used this picture writing. In its most refined stage, ancient Egyptian hieroglyphic writing was a system of signs that stood for the sounds of the spoken language.

Hieroglyphic writing was first used by the Egyptians for carving on stone. Later they initiated a

118

different and simpler form of hieroglyphic writing. They preferred this form for writing on a paperlike material called *papyrus*.

Chinese is one major language that is not written alphabetically. The Chinese language is written in characters. These characters formerly were pictures of objects. Each character today represents a different word or several different words.

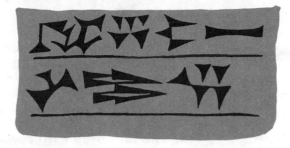

The Japanese language, which is related to the Chinese, also uses no alphabet. In Japanese, each character stands for a syllable or a word.

F-8 Testing Yourself   NUMBER RIGHT

Draw a line under each right answer or fill in each blank.

1. While not directly stated, it can be reasoned from the article that
    a. Egyptians still use picture writing.
    b. the Chinese invented papyrus.
    c. picture writing needs many more characters than are used in most alphabets.

2. This article as a whole is about
    a. picture writing.   c. the ancient Egyptians.
    b. the beginning of the alphabet.   d. Chinese and Japanese writing.

3. The word **they** in paragraph three refers both times to _____.

4. Alphabets are necessary for writing.   Yes   No   Does not say

5. Which two sentences are not true?
    a. Hieroglyphics is a form of alphabet.
    b. The Egyptians invented hieroglyphics.
    c. Papyrus is a kind of stone.
    d. The Chinese write in characters.
    e. Many major languages today are written with alphabets.

6. What word in the last paragraph means **at some time before?**

_____

Getting Ready to Read

SAY AND KNOW	Draw a line under each right answer or fill in the blank.

SAY AND KNOW

rugged
Tibetans
Mongolian
breed
travelers
saddles
dyed
ceremonial
processions
tombs

Draw a line under each right answer or fill in the blank.

1. **Places for the dead** are   **tombs**   **saddles**   **Mongolian.**

2. **Colored with a special liquid** means   **breed**   **dyed**   **rugged.**

3. **Having to do with special things done at special times** means   **rugged**   **Tibetans**   **ceremonial.**

4. **Groups moving forward** are   **breeds**   **processions**   **tombs.**

5. **To develop a kind of animal** is to   **dye**   **saddle**   **breed.**

6. **Those who go from place to place** are _____.

F-9   Camel of Tibet

Tibet is a cold, dry land in Asia bordered on the south by the Himalayas, the highest mountain chain in the world. Native to this rugged land is a wild ox called the yak. A wild yak often stands about 2 meters (6 feet) and may weigh as much as 540 kilograms (1200 pounds). These sturdy creatures may be found living at heights of 500 meters (16,500 feet) above sea level.

The people of Tibet have crossed the wild yak with Mongolian cattle to breed the domestic yak. This animal is so useful to the inhabitants of Tibet that it is doubtful they could survive without it.

In Tibet, the domestic yak carries mail, loads, and travelers. From this animal, the Tibetans get milk and butter. They use its hair to make cloth, mats, and tent coverings. The flesh of the domestic yak is also useful, as it is often dried or roasted and used as food. The yak's hide is made into saddles, whips, and boots. Even the yak's bushy tail is important to the people of the area. It is dyed red and used in ceremonial processions and as an ornament for tombs and shrines.

120

F-9 Testing Yourself

Draw a line under each right answer or fill in each blank.

1. While not directly stated, it can be reasoned from the article that
   a. Tibet does not have a large variety of useful animals.
   b. Tibet now has a modern railroad system.
   c. red dye is made from the blood of the yak.

2. This article as a whole is about
   a. Tibet.   c. a useful animal of Tibet.
   b. India and its neighbors.   d. food made from the flesh of the yak.

3. The word **it** in the last sentence refers to _____.

4. The domestic yak weighs at least 540 kilograms.   Yes   No   Does not say

5. Which two sentences are not true?
   a. Camels are useful in Tibet.   c. Wild yaks are used widely in Tibet.
   b. Yak meat can be eaten.   d. Tibet is north of the Himalayas.
                    e. Domestic yaks carry mail in Tibet.

6. What word in the last paragraph means **decoration?** _____

121

The Electra Mystery

Charles Lindbergh was famous as the first pilot to fly alone over the Atlantic Ocean to Europe. Amelia Earhart was the first female pilot to fly the Atlantic alone.

Earhart was born a traveler. Her father, a lawyer for a railroad, had moved his family to different places often. While living in Canada during World War I, Amelia Earhart became interested in flying.

She watched pilots training for air service. She decided then to learn to fly if she ever got the chance.

During the war, no one could take the time to teach her. But even when peace came, no one would. Then, when the family moved to California, she found a teacher. She paid for her lessons by working for the telephone company.

Before long, Earhart earned her license. She bought a used plane. But there were no jobs for flyers. So she had to take other jobs for a time.

Then came Amelia Earhart's first big chance. In 1928, she was invited to fly along with two men on a trip across the Atlantic on their plane, *Friendship*. It had three engines. It also had pontoons, which allowed it to land and take off on water.

The three pilots left Boston on June 5, 1928. They stopped at Newfoundland. There they stayed for 12 days waiting for good weather. At last they tried to start. But they had to drop 200 of their 900 gallons of gas because the water was so choppy.

They fought heavy rains and strong winds. After 8 hours, their radio went dead. They could not talk with the ships on the sea below them. After 19 hours, they were running out of gas. Anxiously, they looked for land or ships. At

Four years later, Amelia Earhart flew the Atlantic alone. It was not easy. Her plane's altimeter stopped working. Ice formed on the wings during a storm. A fire broke out in the engine. But she made it safely to Ireland in 15 hours.

In 1937, however, Earhart's luck ran out. She and her navigator, Fred Noonan, tried to circle the earth in her plane, *Electra*. They flew from Florida to South America to Africa to New Guinea in the Pacific without trouble. Then on July 2, somewhere near Howland Island, radio distress signals from their plane were picked up. After that came silence. Even today, no one knows what happened.

last they spotted a boat. Then another and another. Then there were a couple of islands. Finally, there appeared a long coastline. It was Wales! The trip had taken them nearly 21 hours.

MY READING TIME _____ (450 WORDS)

Thinking It Over

1. Why do you suppose Amelia Earhart had a hard time finding someone to teach her to fly?

2. Earhart had to go to several different schools because her family moved so much. How do you think this affected her?

3. Do you think we will ever know what happened to Amelia Earhart and Fred Noonan?

Getting Ready to Read

SAY AND KNOW

graceful
distinguishing
stately
mythology
diverse
enable
traditionally
trumpeter
feature
poetry

Draw a line under each right answer or fill in the blank.

1. **To make possible** is to   **enable**   **feature**   **trumpeter.**

2. **Something done according to things handed down from the past** is **done**   **by a trumpeter**   **traditionally.**

3. **Moving with beauty** is **being**   **graceful**   **diverse**   **stately.**

4. **Dignified** means   **stately**   **graceful**   **mythology.**

5. **Making different** means   **distinguishing**   **feature**   **enable.**

6. One country's legends make up its _____ .

G-1 Long-Necked Birds

A long, graceful neck is the main distinguishing feature of stately water birds called swans. Swans have been known for many centuries. They appear in ancient Greek mythology, in fairy tales, and in poetry. In the fifteenth century in England, swans were designated royal birds. Varieties of swans are found in such diverse parts of the world as southern South America and the arctic regions.

Swans may weigh as much as 18 kilograms (40 pounds) and may measure up to 1⅓ meters (4½ feet) long. They live largely on seeds, roots, and fish eggs. The birds' long

necks enable them to reach underwater for food without diving.

Tame swans traditionally are used to ornament ponds and lakes. Wild swans live in flocks, and, in spite of their size and weight, they are able to fly long distances.

The best-known wild swans are whistling swans and trumpeter swans, both of which can be found in the United States. In past decades, the birds were prized by hunters, and many were killed. Conservation efforts have successfully halted the decrease, however, and today these swans are no longer endangered.

G-1   Testing Yourself

NUMBER RIGHT

Draw a line under each right answer or fill in each blank.

1. While not directly stated, it can be reasoned from the article that
    a. flying is difficult for swans.   b. all swans are wild.
      c. swans adjust to both warm and cold climates.

2. This article as a whole is about
    a. the trumpeter swan.   c. facts about swans.
    b. the tame swan.   d. swans in lakes and rivers.

3. The word **their** in the second-to-last sentence refers to _____.

4. In one Greek myth, a god appears as a swan.   Yes   No   Does not say

5. Which two sentences are not true?
    a. Whistling swans are wild.   c. Swans once ruled England.
    b. Trumpeter swans are all tame.   d. Swans appear in old tales.
      e. Swans live in many parts of the world.

6. What word in the first paragraph means **different?** _____

Getting Ready to Read

SAY AND KNOW

skeleton

absorbs

collect

limestone

continual

mammoth

driftwood

decay

evolves

Draw a line under each right answer or fill in the blank.

1. **Soaks up** means **collects** **absorbs** **evolves.**

2. **To gather together** means **to** **continual** **evolve** **collect.**

3. **Wood washed ashore by water** is

                                      mammoth **driftwood** **limestone.**

4. Dead trees are sure to **rot** and **evolve** **decay** **skeleton.**

5. **Something huge** or **gigantic** is

                                    continual **skeleton** **mammoth.**

6. If a form of life develops over a period of time, it

                               _____.

G-2 Skeleton Islands

Some islands are built by small sea animals called corals. Corals live in colonies. They are found only in clean sea water not deeper than about 38 meters (125 feet) and not cooler than 22½°C (68°F). The body of a coral is soft. The animal absorbs limestone from the water and uses this limestone to build hard skeletons about its soft body.

A new coral is formed by a process called *budding*. The young coral grows out of the original coral much in the same way that a new

bud grows out of a plant. The new coral remains attached to the older one. Eventually, the older coral dies, leaving behind only its hard, strong skeleton. In its turn, the

126

young coral gives life to buds, dies, and leaves its skeleton behind.

If this procedure is continued for many, many years, a mammoth structure composed of many layers of coral skeletons, also called coral, reaches the surface of the ocean. When this occurs, seaweed and driftwood collect on top of the structure. In time, they decay and change to earth. Birds stopping on the structure drop seeds, and the growth of plants begins. In this way, a coral island evolves.

G-2 Testing Yourself

Draw a line under each right answer or fill in each blank.

1. While not directly stated, it can be reasoned from the article that
   a. coral islands never reach 30 meters below the ocean's surface.
   b. live corals cannot swim.   c. coral islands are built slowly.

2. This article as a whole is about
   a. how nature works in the ocean.   c. kinds of coral.
   b. the building of a coral island.   d. habits of different sea animals.

3. The word **they** in the third-to-last sentence refers to

   _____.

4. Coral islands are found near the United States.   Yes   No   Does not say.

5. Which two sentences are not true?
   a. Living corals have soft bodies.   c. Coral islands are in clean water.
   b. Corals grow buds.   d. Coral islands are in the Arctic.
       e. Corals cannot live in water that contains limestone.

6. What word in the third paragraph means repeated many times?

   _____

Getting Ready to Read

SAY AND KNOW

human

layer

waxy

flipper

suggest

streak

fin

lens

related

Draw a line under each right answer or fill in the blank.

1. It is found on fish and sea animals.   **fin**   **lens**   **human**

2. **Another part of a fish or sea animal** is **a**
   related   **flipper**   **suggest.**

3. It can make things look larger when you look through it.
   related   **flipper**   **lens**

4. Something that looks and feels like wax is
   layer   **streak**   **waxy.**

5. **People** are   **human**   **layer**   **streak.**

6. Members of a family are —————————————— to each other.

G-3   How Are They Like Us?

Whales seem to be related to human beings. The bones in a whale's flipper look much like those in a human hand. Do they live about as long as humans?

It is hard to tell. We do not see whales being born, except in captivity. We cannot follow them through their lives and know when they die.

An English scientist, Christina Lockyer, has suggested a possible way to tell. She counted the layers in the waxy plugs in the ear canal of the whale. The whale's ear openings are very small. They are about the size of a pencil lead. Dr. Lockyer used a hand lens to see dark and light streaks in the ear plug. Each pair of streaks is one year's deposit. Counting the streaks let her know about how long the whale had lived.

Fin whales have been found to live as long as 80 years, about as long as human beings.

Like human beings, whales live in groups and communicate with each other using sounds called phonations. Microphones have picked up phonations over a distance of 50 miles (80 km).

G-3 Testing Yourself

NUMBER RIGHT

Draw a line under each right answer or fill in each blank.

1. While not directly stated, it may be reasoned from the article that
    a. many human beings live to be 80 years old.
    b. small whales are not hunted.
    c. a whale's eyes are like those of a human being.

2. This article as a whole is about
    a. killing whales.
    b. the birth of whales.
    c. the bones in a whale's flipper.
    d. how whales and human beings are alike.

3. The word **those** in the first paragraph, second sentence, refers to

    _____.

4. A whale's ear opening is about the size of a pencil lead.   Yes   No   Does not say

5. Which two sentences are not true?
    a. Christina Lockyer is an English scientist.
    b. Whales' ears have streaks in them that can be counted.
    c. Whales do not have very long lives.
    d. Whales and human beings are alike in some ways.
    e. Layers of skin tell how old a whale is.

6. What word in the second paragraph means **caged** or **fenced in**?

    _____

Getting Ready to Read

carbon
recognized
greasy
streaks
deposits
lubricants
consistency
specified
inserted
grooves
hollows

Draw a line under each right answer or fill in the blank.

1. **Put in** means   **grooves**   **carbon**   **inserted.**

2. **Materials laid down by nature** are   **deposits**   **streaks**   **greasy.**

3. **Empty places** are called   **carbons**   **hollows**   **lubricants.**

4. **Something named** is   **inserted**   **specified**   **streaked.**

5. **The amount of firmness** is called **the**   **carbon**   **greasy**   **consistency.**

6. Something known again has been _____.

G-4   Not a Lead Pencil

It is quite a surprise to many people to learn that there is no lead in the common lead pencil. The black substance is graphite, which is often called "black lead." This name is not a suitable one, however, because graphite is nearly pure carbon and contains no lead.

Graphite is one of the softest of all minerals. It is dark gray to black in color and can be recognized by its greasy feel, its softness, and the black streaks that it makes. It is very widely distributed over the earth but is not often found in large deposits.

Graphite is used in making lubricants—that is, substances used

130

to reduce friction. It is also used in making lead pencils, stove blacking, paints, and many other things.

When used for making pencils, the graphite is first ground into a powder. It is then mixed with pipe clay and water. This mixture is ground again. When it reaches the proper consistency, the paste is forced through small holes and comes out as strings. These strings are baked, cut into specified lengths, and inserted into the grooves or hollows in the pencils.

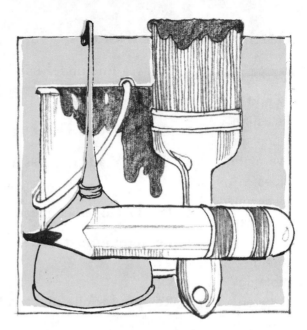

G-4 Testing Yourself

NUMBER RIGHT

Draw a line under each right answer or fill in each blank.

1. While not directly stated, it can be reasoned from the article that
    a. graphite is like lead.   b. graphite is never found in large deposits.
        c. a better name for "lead" pencils would be "carbon" pencils.

2. This article as a whole is about
    a. the uses of graphite.   c. how pencils are made.
    b. carbon.   d. why pencils should be made with lead.

3. The word **it** in the second paragraph, last sentence, refers to

_____.

4. Graphite is softer than lead.   Yes   No   Does not say

5. Which two sentences are not true?
    a. Graphite contains mostly lead.   c. Some lubricants are made of graphite.
    b. Graphite is a hard mineral.   d. Graphite contains no lead.
        e. Graphite is found in many parts of the earth.

6. What word in paragraph two means **spread?** _____

Getting Ready to Read

SAY AND KNOW   Draw a line under each right answer or fill in the blank.

legend
Palestine
astonished
overnight
clues
glassmaking
glassware
combining
foreign
molding
Babylon

1. **A tale** or **story** is **a**   **Palestine**   **clue**   **legend.**

2. **To be very surprised** is **to be**   **foreign**   **astonished**   **molding.**

3. **Things made of glass** are called

                      glassmaking   **Babylon**   **glassware.**

4. **Putting together** means   **molding**   **overnight**   **combining.**

5. **Something that doesn't belong** may be called

                      Babylon   **clues**   **foreign.**

6. **To stay for one night** is **to stay** _____.

G-5   Soda, Lime, and Sand

According to legend, some Phoenician sailors once became lost in a storm and landed on the coast of Palestine. Having built a fire on the sandy beach, they placed their cooking pots on blocks of nitron, a substance which contains soda. In the morning, it is said, the astonished

132

sailors found rough pieces of glass that had been made overnight by the sand and soda melting together in the heat of the fire. This story may not be true, but it may give us clues about the beginnings of glassmaking.

Today we make glass by combining soda, lime, and sand. A mixture of these elements is heated to 1427°C (2600°F). At this very high temperature, the mixture becomes liquid. After this, all foreign matter is removed from the mixture, and the hot liquid is allowed to cool. Once it cools, it is ready for molding into different shapes.

Glass blowing, which is the ancient art of forming glass by blowing it through a tube, was practiced thousands of years ago in Egypt, Babylon, and China. Today most glassware is not blown but is made by machines in factories.

G-5 Testing Yourself

NUMBER RIGHT

Draw a line under each right answer or fill in each blank.

1. While not directly stated, it can be reasoned from the article that
   - a. it may be that glass was first developed by accident.
   - b. only cold glass can be molded into different shapes.
   - c. no glass is blown today.

2. This article as a whole is about
   - a. the origin of glassmaking.
   - b. the place of legend in history.
   - c. the making of glass.
   - d. a very useful article.

3. The word **they** in the first paragraph, second sentence, refers to

   _____.

4. The art of blowing glass has been lost.   Yes   No   Does not say

5. Which two sentences are not true?
   - a. Most glass today is made by machine.
   - b. Foreign matter is removed from glass after it cools.
   - c. Glass blowing was known in ancient Egypt.
   - d. The sailors in the story landed on the shores of Greece.
   - e. Nitron blocks once were used under cooking pots.

6. What word in the last paragraph means **carried on?** _____

Getting Ready to Read

SAY AND KNOW

nations
ambassadors
codes
ciphers
receivers
encode
decode
exchange
cryptographers
invented
substitution
zinc
complex

Draw a line under each right answer or fill in the blank.

1. It is the **opposite of simple.**   zinc   code   complex

2. It means **to make something new.**   exchange   decode   invent

3. **People who solve ciphers** are

        cryptographers   ambassadors   receivers.

4. One **way to write a secret message** is with **a**

        nation   cipher   receiver.

5. It means **replacement.**   substitution   code   cipher

6. When you write a message in a secret language, you

        _____ it.

G-6 Keeping Secrets

For as long as nations have been sending each other ambassadors, the ambassadors have been sending home messages in codes or ciphers. Codes and ciphers are both ways to hide the meaning of a message. With a code, senders and receivers agree ahead of time that a certain word will be used instead of another word or word group. They might decide, for example, that *phone* stands for *meeting* and *Mark* means *Tuesday*. The message "Phone Mark" tells the receiver that the meeting is Tuesday. People who use codes need to have code books in order to encode or decode messages.

With ciphers, the letters in a word are scrambled or replaced by other letters. Every *m* might be changed to *c* and every *z* to *p*, and so forth. A message using a one-for-one exchange is fairly easy to break. To keep messages secret, cryptographers have invented increasingly complicated ciphers. They might, for example, mix several systems of letter substitution in one message.

People using ciphers do not need to have special books. Anybody who has the key giving the letter replacements can send and receive messages. People who do not have the key can use these language facts to break the code: *E* is the most frequently used letter in English. It is followed by *t, a, o, n, i, r, s,* then *h.* The least used letters are *q* and *z.* You can count how often each letter is used to help decode the message. Of course, this system won't always work. Suppose the message is about zinc in Zanzibar!

Even before computers, inventors created machines that made very complex ciphers. These ciphers were harder to break. But machines could also be used to crack them. With computers, ever more complicated ciphers are being developed. Every time a new cipher comes out of a computer, someone at another computer looks for a way to break it!

G-6   Testing Yourself

Draw a line under each right answer or fill in each blank.

1. While not directly stated, it can be reasoned from the article that
   a. secret messages are important only in times of war.
   b. American ciphers cannot be decoded by people in other countries.
   c. our government employs people to create and to break ciphers.

2. The article as a whole is about
   a. codes and ciphers.
   b. computers.
   c. the alphabet.
   d. secret languages.

3. The word **they** in the first paragraph refers to _____.

4. No cipher has ever been invented that cannot be solved.   Yes   No   Does not say

5. Which two sentences are not true?
   a. The letter *t* is one of the most used in the English language.
   b. Governments have been using codes and ciphers for centuries.
   c. The most used letter in a cipher always stands for *e.*
   d. A code is just about the same as a cipher.
   e. Computers are important tools for cryptographers.

6. Which word in the third paragraph means **often**? _____

Getting Ready to Read

population
mighty
Amazon River
contributing
tropical
abundant
foliage
unhealthy
advances
enabled
resources
deposit

Draw a line under each right answer or fill in the blank.

1. **Something large and very strong** can be called
   abundant   unhealthy   mighty.

2. **Another word for donating or joining** is
   contributing   advancing   enabling.

3. **Made possible** means   **considered   used   enabled**.

4. **The opposite of well** is   **unhealthy   abundant   resources**.

5. **Leaves** are   **resources   unhealthy   foliage**.

6. **More than enough** means _____.

G-7   Coffee Riches

Almost half of the whole continent of South America is taken up by one country, Brazil. While its population is much less than that of the United States, Brazil's area is almost as large. Two of the largest cities in the world, Rio de Janeiro (6 million) and São Paulo (11 million), are in Brazil.

The mighty Amazon River, with its 200 contributing streams, is the world's largest river system. Part of it flows through Brazil. Along the river's shores is the world's largest tropical forest, in which grows varied and abundant foliage.

The climate in this part of

Brazil has for a long time been considered unhealthy for people. Recent advances in medicine, however, have enabled doctors to fight many of the diseases. Because of this, they are now able to live and work in the land.

Brazil would be a very rich country if all its resources could be used. Gold, diamonds, valuable trees, and the world's largest single deposit of iron are found in Brazil. Rubber and sugar are produced there as well. And Brazil exports 1/4 of the world's supply of coffee. But Brazil's chief source of wealth does not lie in its varied resources. Today, factories and service industries contribute the most to Brazil's wealth.

G-7   Testing Yourself

Draw a line under each right answer or fill in each blank.

1. While not directly stated, it can be reasoned from the article that
   a. Brazil produces much iron.   b. no one farms along the Amazon.
      c. more people live along the Amazon today than ever before.

2. This article as a whole is about
   a. a poor country.   c. a country rich in resources.
   b. a country with many people.   d. the Amazon River Valley.

3. The word **its** in the second paragraph, first sentence, refers to

   _____   _____.

4. Lumber is Brazil's chief source of wealth.   Yes   No   Does not say

5. Which two sentences are not true?
   a. Brazil could be a rich country.
   b. Diamonds are found in Brazil.
   c. Brazil is the same size as the United States.
   d. Coffee is raised in Brazil.
   e. All of the Amazon River is found in Brazil.

6. What word in the third paragraph means **made lately?** _____

Getting Ready to Read

SAY AND KNOW

accomplishment

historians

Semitic

recording

scholars

simplified

foundation

phases

evolution

Draw a line under each right answer or fill in the blank.

1. **The process of developing slowly** is called

                           Semitic   evolution   phases.

2. **Those who study the happenings of the past** are called

                         phases   historians   recordings.

3. **The base** is called   **the foundation   scholars   historians.**

4. It means **writing down.**   **phases   simplified   recording**

5. **Made less difficult** is   **simplified   phases   foundation.**

6. It means **something that has been completed.**

                                _____

G-8   The First Alphabet

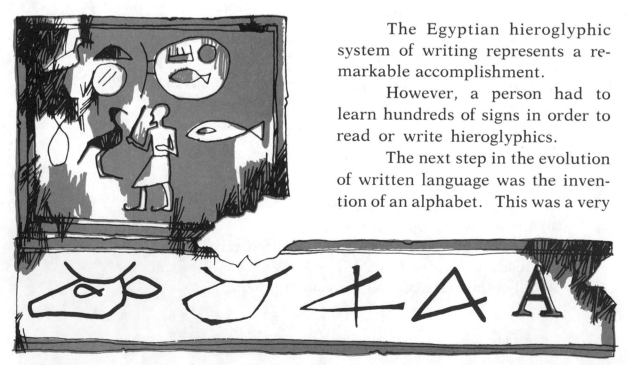

The Egyptian hieroglyphic system of writing represents a remarkable accomplishment.

However, a person had to learn hundreds of signs in order to read or write hieroglyphics.

The next step in the evolution of written language was the invention of an alphabet. This was a very difficult process and probably a very slow one. Language historians believe that the step was first taken by an ancient Semitic people. Gradually, they were able to develop a system of recording language that became the earliest known alphabet.

Scholars have described a number of phases that must have been part of this development. For example, in writing about an ox, these people first used a picture of an ox. Afterwards, the picture was simplified into a sign signifying ox. Then the sign came to stand for the sounds made when the word ox was pronounced. Finally, the sign or character stood for a sound alone. Only when this stage was reached was the real foundation for an alphabet laid.

These early alphabet-makers used 22 such characters in their alphabet. With these few characters, they were able to form thousands of words.

G-8   Testing Yourself   NUMBER RIGHT

Draw a line under each right answer or fill in each blank.

1. While not directly stated, it can be reasoned from the article that
   a. the Egyptians finally developed the first alphabet.
   b. even scholars are not sure who developed the first alphabet.
   c. in an alphabet, a few signs can form many words.

2. This article as a whole is about
   a. hieroglyphics.
   b. language historians.
   c. how signs became language.
   d. part of the evolution of written language.

3. The word **their** in the last paragraph refers to _____.

4. The first alphabet probably had 22 characters.   Yes   No   Does not say

5. Which two sentences are not true?
   a. Inventing an alphabet was difficult.
   b. The ox was unknown to the ancients.
   c. Some scholars study language.
   d. Language cannot be recorded.
   e. Hieroglyphics are not letters.

6. What word in the fourth paragraph means **standing for**?

Getting Ready to Read

outstanding

enroll

encourage

medal

patients

succeed

medical

college

medicine

Draw a line under each right answer or fill in the blank.

1. It means **to be able to do what you want.**

enroll   medical   succeed

2. **To sign up for school** is to   medal   enroll   encourage.

3. When you study to be a doctor, you study

medicine   outstanding   succeed.

4. **A circular piece of metal given as a reward** is a

medal   college   enroll.

5. **People treated by doctors** are   patients   students   outstanding.

6. **The opposite of dishearten** is _____.

G-9   A Nurse but Not a Doctor?

"You can be a nurse but not a doctor." This is what Elizabeth Blackwell heard in 1847 when she tried to enroll in medical school.

She had decided to be a doctor when a friend was ill. Her friend wished she had had a woman for a doctor. The young woman felt it would have been easier to talk to another woman. She encouraged Elizabeth Blackwell to study medicine.

To get money for medical college, Elizabeth Blackwell taught school. The principal had once been a doctor. Part of Blackwell's pay was to be allowed to study the principal's books. She later worked for another doctor and read his medical books also.

At first, no school would take her. Finally, the Medical College of Geneva, New York, did. She became the first woman in the United States to attend such a college. After Geneva, she went to Paris for more training. There, she was allowed to attend classes only if she dressed like a man!

She returned home in 1851. No one would rent an office to her at first. Patients were slow to go to a woman doctor. But finally Blackwell and her sister succeeded in starting a hospital for women.

Today the Blackwell medal is given to outstanding women in medicine.

G-9   Testing Yourself

Draw a line under each right answer or fill in each blank.

1. While not directly stated, it can be reasoned from the article that
   a. it is now easy for women to become doctors.
   b. female doctors probably understand women patients better than male doctors do.
   c. today as many women are doctors as are nurses.

2. This article as a whole is about
   a. the first American woman to become a doctor.
   b. medical colleges in America.
   c. the first American woman to become a nurse.
   d. studying to be a doctor.

3. The word **she** in the second paragraph, second sentence, refers to

   _____   _____.

4. All nurses today are women.   Yes   No   Does not say

5. Which two sentences are not true?
   a. Elizabeth Blackwell studied medicine in London.
   b. The Blackwell medal is given to the best doctor each year.
   c. Blackwell got part of her education by reading medical books by herself.
   d. Blackwell once taught school.
   e. Blackwell and her sister started a hospital for women.

6. What word in the last sentence means **one of the best?**

   _____

Sir Gawain's Marriage

Once King Arthur found himself in the power of a bold baron. The King had entered an enchanted forest owned by the baron, and, because of the enchantment, had been unable to defend himself when the baron rode against him.

The baron offered to spare King Arthur's life if, in the space of one year, Arthur could return with the answer to this question: What does every woman want most? King Arthur agreed to do so.

Arthur asked many people for the answer. Some told him it was beauty. Others said jewels. Still others said flattery or power. The months passed, and Arthur was unable to find the answer to the baron's question. Finally, at the end of the year, King Arthur rode back toward the enchanted forest. As he neared the place, he heard a voice say, "King Arthur, stop! I will help you."

Turning, Arthur beheld the ugliest woman he had ever seen. The King could barely hide his horror, but he politely thanked her and said he feared that no one could help him. The hag promised to give him the answer to the question if he would grant her one request. Arthur promised and listened to the answer she whispered in his ear.

"Of course!" cried the delighted king. "Now tell me what I can do for you."

"I will tell you when you return to court," she said.

Arthur rode confidently to meet the baron. "You may have three chances to answer my question," the baron told him. "What is the answer?"

"Is it beauty?" asked Arthur. The baron shook his head.

"Is it wealth?" asked Arthur. Again the baron shook his head.

"Then," said Arthur triumphantly, "what every woman wishes must be her own will!" The baron was enraged, but he kept his word and freed the King.

Arthur returned to court and asked the woman for her request. When she asked to marry one of his knights, he was filled with horror. He told the story to the knights, who remained silent. Finally, Sir Gawain said he would marry her. Everyone was shocked, for Gawain was young and very handsome. Gawain, however, was determined to help the King, and he married the ugly woman.

After the guests had left, Gawain's bride said, "Gawain, look at me." He lifted his eyes. There stood the most beautiful lady he had ever seen. She told him that he saw her now in her true form. She had been enchanted and had needed to marry a gallant knight to break the spell.

When Gawain led this lovely lady before Arthur and his knights, their sadness turned to joy, and a great wedding feast was held.

MY READING TIME _____ **(450 WORDS)**

Thinking It Over

1. Why did Arthur not give the correct answer first?

2. Why did Arthur return after the year's time, when he knew the baron would kill him?

3. What can you learn from this story?

Getting Ready to Read

Draw a line under each right answer or fill in the blank.

normal

ostrich

dissolve

amazing

examination

appetite

doubtful

stomach

consider

1. It means **surprising.**   normal   amazing   doubtful

2. It means about the same as **melt.**   dissolve   appetite   stomach

3. If you are **not sure,** you are   doubtful   ostrich   consider.

4. It is **an inspection** or **investigation.**

    appetite   examination   dissolve

5. It means **to think** or **believe.**   to consider   amazing   examination

6. If a thing is **regular** or **usual,** it is _____.

H-1   Good or Bad?

Many birds eat seeds and fruit. Most eat insects. The bird with the most amazing appetite is the ostrich. Inside one ostrich, after it died in a Florida zoo, were found bottle caps, a thimble, a golf ball, a teething ring, and three pennies!

People have often judged birds to be good or bad by what they eat. For example, birds that eat insects, like flies and grasshoppers, are considered "good." They are thought to be helpful to farmers. But many insects are needed by human beings. If there were no insects, we would have no fruit to eat. Birds also eat some insects which kill other, more harmful insects.

Owls and hawks, on the other hand, are frequently thought to be "bad." Some farmers believe they kill chickens. But it is doubtful that they do. When such birds kill and eat small animals, they swallow them whole. The strong stomach juices dissolve everything but the fur and bones, which are spit up as "pellets." Examination of such pellets has usually shown that mice and squirrels, but not chickens, have been eaten.

Sometimes, hawks and owls do attack and frighten chickens. But often this happens because the farmers have poisoned the squirrels and mice, the normal food of these birds.

H-1 Testing Yourself

NUMBER RIGHT

Draw a line under each right answer or fill in each blank.

1. While not directly stated, it can be reasoned from the article that
   a. birds are neither "good" nor "bad" but are just birds.
   b. all insects are enemies of human beings.
   c. all ostriches will eat pennies and dimes.

2. This article as a whole is about
   a. birds that eat insects.   c. what an ostrich eats.
   b. "good" and "bad" birds.   d. hawks and owls.

3. The word **they** in the second paragraph, third sentence, refers to

   _____.

4. Eagles sometimes kill and eat chickens.   Yes   No   Does not say

5. Which two sentences are not true?
   a. Some birds eat mice.
   b. Pellets are what birds spit up.
   c. Owls prefer to eat seeds and insects.
   d. Flies are insects.
   e. Hawks have never frightened chickens.

6. What word in the first paragraph means **a place where animals are on display?**

   _____

Getting Ready to Read

Draw a line under each right answer or fill in the blank.

1. **Things that take place** are **happenings** **portions** **zenith**.

2. **Arcs** are **wavering** **curves** **streamers**.

3. It means **part**. **zenith** **occurrence** **portion**

4. **The act of receiving** is **reception** **occurrence** **trembling**.

5. **The highest point** is called **the** **streamer** **Siberia** **zenith**.

6. **Long, flowing things** are called _____.

H-2 Nature's Electric Lights

One of Earth's most beautiful sights is the aurora borealis, or northern lights. These lights appear only at night and are most often seen in far-northern lands. Occasionally, they may be seen as far south as the northern United States. In Alaska, Siberia, and northern Canada the occurrence of the aurora borealis may appear as often as a hundred times in a single year.

The northern lights are electric in nature. Because of this, they may sometimes interfere with radio and television reception. The aurora borealis is most often seen when there are many spots on the sun. Thus, it is probable that bombardment of the upper atmosphere by particles from the sun causes the lights.

Here is a description of the northern lights written by someone who saw them from Siberia. "The whole universe seemed to be on fire. A broad arch of brilliant colors spanned the heavens from east to

146

west, with a fringe of crimson and yellow streamers stretching up to the zenith. Every portion of the vast arch was wavering, trembling, and changing color. The brilliant streamers swept back and forth in great curves."

H-2 Testing Yourself

NUMBER RIGHT

Draw a line under each right answer or fill in each blank.

1. While not directly stated, it can be reasoned from the article that
a. northern lights show daily.   b. northern lights are not seen in Mexico.
c. northern lights are seen more often in Canada than Alaska.

2. This article as a whole is about
a. nature's beauty.   c. something in history.
b. a beautiful sight.   d. the wonders of electric lights.

3. The word **they** in sentence three refers to _____.

4. Aurora borealis and northern lights are somewhat different in meaning.

Yes   No   Does not say

5. Which two sentences are not true?
a. Northern lights are electrical.
b. Northern lights may be related to sunspots.
c. Northern lights never are seen south of Canada.
d. Northern lights never appear more than twice each year.
e. Northern lights may interfere with television reception.

6. What words in the second paragraph mean **get in the way of?**

_____   _____

147

Getting Ready to Read

snake
cycle
transparent
transparency
required
journey
parents
upstream
instinctively
assume

Draw a line under each right answer or fill in the blank.

1. **A round of events** is **a**   **cycle   snake   journey.**

2. Window glass is   **instinctively   snake   transparent.**

3. **Something needed** is   **upstream   assumed   required.**

4. **Fathers and mothers** are   **parents   a transparency   a cycle.**

5. **To take for granted** means **to   assume   journey   require.**

6. Most people avoid danger _____ .

H-3   Glass Fish

An eel is a long fish that looks more like a snake than a fish. Eels swim like water snakes but are capable of traveling much faster. Some varieties of eel spend all of their time in salt water. The most common kinds of eel, however, are those that also live in fresh water.

The life cycle of a freshwater eel starts far out in the ocean where the female eel has deposited her eggs. When first hatched, the baby eel is transparent, very thin, and

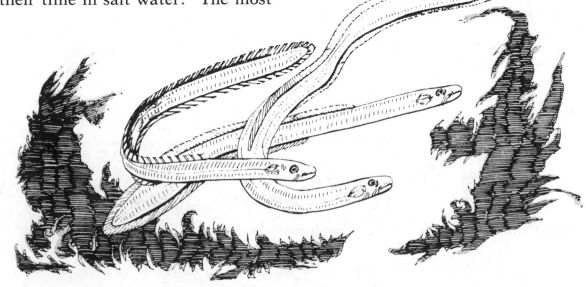

shaped somewhat like a leaf. Because of its transparency, a baby eel is called a glass fish.

After they hatch, these glass fish begin swimming toward land. Two to three years are required for their journey. Toward the end of this time, the glass fish assume a new shape and begin to look more like their parents. Finally, they leave the ocean and swim upstream in fresh water.

After this, eels spend most of their lives in rivers and ponds. When they are ready to lay their eggs, however, the female eels instinctively start for the sea. Only when they have reached the ocean region where they were born do they lay eggs.

H-3 Testing Yourself

NUMBER RIGHT

Draw a line under each right answer or fill in each blank.

1. While not directly stated, it can be reasoned from the article that
   a. no eel lives entirely in fresh water.   b. eels are really snakes.
            c. grown eels are called glass fish.

2. This article as a whole is about
   a. eels.   c. water snakes.
   b. freshwater eels.   d. snakes and glass fish.

3. The word **they** in the third paragraph, fourth sentence, refers to

   _____   _____.

4. Some eels spend their whole lives in salt water.   Yes   No   Does not say

5. Which two sentences are not true?
   a. Snakes are called glass fish.   c. Baby eels are transparent.
   b. Eels lay their eggs in ponds.   d. Eels can swim upstream.
            e. The eel looks much like the snake.

6. What word in the last paragraph means **area?** _____

Getting Ready to Read

SAY AND KNOW

Draw a line under each right answer or fill in the blank.

mineral

resistance

consumption

properties

corrosion

clog

combine

reclaim

consequently

1. It means **to restore.**   clog   corrosion   reclaim

2. **Rust** is a kind of   **properties   corrosion   consumption.**

3. Something that is mined is a   **clog   mineral   resistance.**

4. It means **to join one thing to another.**
   resistance   mineral   combine

5. It means **as a result of.**   reclaim   consequently   combine

6. When you oppose something, you are showing _____ to it.

H-4   The Earliest Metal

Copper was the first important metal used widely by human beings. It was first used about 8,000 years ago for weapons and tools. It has been greatly prized by all people since then. Except for gold, reddish-brown copper is the only metal with a color other than a shade of gray.

Three properties of copper continue to make it valuable today. Copper wire is an excellent conductor of electricity. Copper also is a good conductor of heat and is used in refrigerators and heating coils. Finally, it is highly resistant to corrosion. Copper pipe, unlike iron pipe, does not clog easily because it does not pick up mineral deposits readily.

Copper combines well with other metals. Bronze is a mixture of copper and tin. Brass, combining copper and zinc, is used in industry for its superior strength and resistance to corrosion. Monel, which is 60 percent copper and 40 percent nickel, is sometimes even more resistant to corrosion than stainless steel.

The United States at present uses more copper than it produces. In fact, the United States uses more copper than any other country in the world. World consumption of copper is greater than production. Consequently, there is increased use of copper which is reclaimed from trimmings and sweepings.

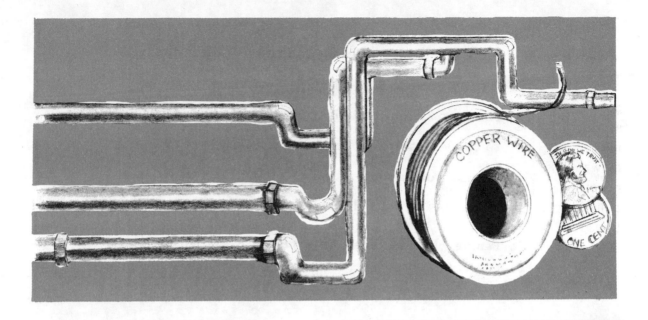

H-4 Testing Yourself

Draw a line under each right answer or fill in each blank.

1. While not directly stated, it can be reasoned from the article that
    a. we may soon have to find a substitute for copper.
    b. copper was once considered more valuable than gold.
    c. copper is different from all other metals only because it is not gray.

2. This article as a whole is about
    a. a reddish-brown metal.   c. resistance to corrosion.
    b. the need for a substitute for copper.   d. conductors of electricity.

3. The word **it** in the second sentence refers to ＿＿＿＿＿＿＿＿＿＿＿＿＿.

4. Monel is more valuable than copper.   Yes   No   Does not say

5. Which two sentences are not true?
    a. Copper was first used about 8000 years ago.
    b. Copper is gray in color.
    c. The United States is able to produce all the copper it needs.
    d. Copper pipe does not clog easily.
    e. Monel sometimes resists corrosion better than stainless steel.

6. What word in the first paragraph means **valued?** ＿＿＿＿＿＿＿＿＿＿＿＿＿

151

Getting Ready to Read

SAY AND KNOW

design
government
service
pilots
crews
private
airlines
transport
stimulus

Draw a line under each right answer or fill in the blank.

1. It quickens action. **stimulus   services   airlines**

2. **The opposite of public** is   **pilot   private   transport.**

3. **To carry** means to   **design   transport   stimulus.**

4. **Groups working together** are   **pilots   service   crews.**

5. **Form** may mean   **design   private   government.**

6. **People who steer boats or airplanes** are called _____.

H-5   Mail by Air

A stimulus to progress in aviation came with the beginning of airmail service by the United States government. Changes in structure and design of the planes to carry airmail were necessary. Large amounts of money were needed. Such money was provided when Congress gave the Postmaster General authority to carry mail at a rate not more than $3.00 per pound (.45 kilogram).

The airmail service began on May 15, 1918. It flew between Washington, D.C., and New York City. The planes, pilots, and ground crews were supplied by the army. By August 12 of the same year, the Post Office Department had com-

pletely taken over the airmail service by furnishing its own planes and crews. In 1925, however, an act of

152

Congress transferred airmail service to private airlines.

From its small beginning, airmail and transport service have grown into a great business. Very little first-class mail is carried any longer by train. Almost all first-class mail going 640 kilometers (400 miles) or more within the country is now being sent by airmail.

Airmail service has also progressed in other countries throughout the world. Today, airmail service is available to almost any part of the earth.

H-5 Testing Yourself

NUMBER RIGHT

Draw a line under each right answer or fill in each blank.

1. While not directly stated, it can be reasoned from the article that
   a. all first-class mail is now sent by plane.
   b. it would not be worth it to send first-class mail 320 kilometers (200 miles) by plane.
   c. the army ran the airmail service better than the Post Office Department.

2. This article as a whole is about
   a. changes made in planes to carry airmail.
   b. pilots and ground crews.
   c. the development of airmail service.
   d. airmail service in other countries.

3. The word **it** in the second paragraph, second sentence, refers to

   _____ _____.

4. The United States Army once ran the airmail service.   Yes   No   Does not say

5. Which two sentences are not true?
   a. Not many other countries have airmail service.
   b. Airmail service began in 1918.
   c. Trains carry little first-class mail.
   d. Airmail service is a big business.
   e. Today the Post Office Department flies the airmail planes.

6. What word in the last paragraph means **gone forward** or **grown?**

   _____

Getting Ready to Read

therefore
convenient
uncertain
goddess
worshipped
Norse
Teutonic
thunder
deities
Thor
Tyr
Frigg
Woden

Draw a line under each right answer or fill in the blank.

1. **Therefore** means **as a** **result** **cause** **matter of fact.**

2. **The opposite of sure** is **Tyr** **convenient** **uncertain.**

3. **A female god** is called **a** **goddess** **Teutonic** **Thor.**

4. **Gods** may also be called **thunder** **deities** **Woden.**

5. **The time or space between two events** is
   deities **the interval** **worshipped.**

6. Something _____ saves time and work.

H-6 A Convenient Measure

The week as a measure of time does not depend on the movement of the moon or the Earth. It is therefore different from the day, the month, and the year. The week is a convenient interval, used because it is necessary to have a measure of time longer than a day but shorter than a month.

The beginning of the 7-day week is uncertain. The Babylonians had no week, and the early Romans had an 8-day week.

In many languages, the names for the 7 days of the week were derived from the names of the deities worshiped by the ancients. At one time, it was believed that the god of

the sun was in charge of one day, the goddess of the moon of another, and so on. Thus, in English, Sunday is sun's day; Monday, moon's day; and Saturday, the day of the Roman god Saturn. Tuesday is named for the Norse god of war, Tyr, and Wednesday for Woden, the chief Teutonic god. Thursday is the day of Thor, the Norse god of thunder, while Friday is named for Frigg, the Norse goddess of love.

H-6   Testing Yourself

NUMBER RIGHT

Draw a line under each right answer or fill in each blank.

1. While not directly stated, it can be reasoned from the article that
   a. Woden was more powerful in Norse myths than was Tyr.
   b. the Babylonians created the week.
   c. the movement of the earth determines the week's length.

2. This article as a whole is about
   a. Teutonic gods.   c. measures of time made by humans.
   b. the goddess of love.   d. the Roman god Saturn.

3. The word **it** in the second sentence refers to _____.

4. Frigg was a Roman goddess.   Yes   No   Does not say

5. Which two sentences are not true?
   a. The month is based on the movement of the sun.
   b. Our week consists of 7 days.
   c. Babylonians had no week.
   d. Tuesday is named for Teuton.
   e. The early Roman week was 8 days long.

6. What word in the third paragraph means **having to do with an ancient Germanic**

   tribe? _____

Getting Ready to Read

SAY AND KNOW   Draw a line under each right answer or fill in the blank.

endure

elderberry

stifling

splints

gargle

patients

prevent

broth

cleansing

feverish

infection

1. Disease caused by germs is   **infection**   **gargle**   **elderberry.**

2. **To undergo** or **bear** means **to**   **gargle**   **endure**   **broth.**

3. It means **making clean.**   **prevent**   **stifling**   **cleansing**

4. **People being treated for illness** are called

                               splints   **feverish**   **patients.**

5. **To keep something from happening** is **to**

                                 prevent it   **splint it**   **broth.**

6. **A liquid used for washing the throat** is a _____.

H-7   More than Magic

Although Native Americans believed in magic for curing illness, they also had some effective, almost modern, ways of treating patients. The sweat house, for example, was used to treat many illnesses, and in cases of fever where sweating was desirable, this treatment proved very helpful.

The sweat house was a dirt-covered hut in which a fire was kept burning. When a feverish person entered, the single door would be closed tight. The person would remain in the hut and endure the stifling heat for as long as possible. Then, this person would run outside and complete the treatment by leaping into the nearest lake or stream.

In addition to such extreme treatments, Native Americans were skilled in setting broken bones and putting them in splints and in cleansing wounds to prevent infection.

Native Americans also used many wild plants for medicines. From lizard tail, they made a gargle for sore throats; from wild peony, they made a medicine administered for stomach aches; and from elderberry blossoms, they made a broth to cure fevers. Some of the many drugs Native Americans obtained from plants are still in use today.

H-7 Testing Yourself

Draw a line under each right answer or fill in each blank.

1. While not directly stated, it can be reasoned from the article that
   a. modern medicine could use some methods from Native American people.
   b. Native Americans had no way to cure sick people.
   c. none of the Native Americans' drugs were effective.

2. This article as a whole is about
   a. sweat houses.
   b. Native American medicine.
   c. lizard tails and gargles.
   d. broth for fevers.

3. The word **them** in the third paragraph refers to _____.

4. Sweat houses were good for curing measles.   Yes   No   Does not say

5. Which two sentences are not true?
   a. Native Americans could prevent infection.
   b. Sweat houses were cold places.
   c. Native Americans made medicines.
   d. Native Americans could set broken bones.
   e. Native Americans needed nothing but magic for curing illness.

6. What word in the third paragraph means **making clean?**

Getting Ready to Read

SAY AND KNOW

Syria

consonants

accounts

modified

prior

perfected

alphabetic

inaugurated

necessity

Draw a line under each right answer or fill in the blank.

1. **Changed slightly** means **consonants** **alphabetic** **modified.**

2. **Before** means **prior** **accounts** **necessity.**

3. **Having to do with a system of letters** means

                                      necessity **alphabetic** **Syria.**

4. **Explanations** are usually **necessities** **accounts** **consonants.**

5. It means **introduced** or **begun.**

                              accounts **perfected** **inaugurated**

6. When **all faults have been removed,** a thing is said to be

                                            _____.

H-8   Early Alphabets

The ancient Egyptian system of writing, called hieroglyphics, became known to the Semites, a people then living in Syria and Palestine. Between the years 1500 and 1000 B.C., the Semites developed an alphabetic writing of their own. They invented their own set of characters, which stood for the consonants in their language.

About this time in ancient history, people were beginning to trade with one another. Ships were used in increasing numbers to transport goods from one place to another. When the goods were sold or traded, accurate written accounts became necessary. A simple written language was becoming a necessity.

By about 1000 B.C., a people called the Phoenicians had inaugurated a 22-character alphabet. In their travels, Phoenician traders came in contact with the Greeks. The Greeks borrowed Phoenician characters, modified them, and used them to form the Greek alphabet. All this happened sometime prior to 800 B.C. Much later, the Greeks modified and changed their system to form a 24-letter alphabet.

The Romans put the finishing touches on this system. It is the 26-letter alphabet, perfected by the Romans, that we use today.

H-8   Testing Yourself

NUMBER RIGHT

Draw a line under each right answer or fill in each blank.

1. While not directly stated, it can be reasoned from the article that
   a. our alphabet comes directly from the Greeks.
   b. over hundreds of years, many ancient peoples helped build our alphabet.
   c. the Semites developed hieroglyphics.

2. This article as a whole is about
   a. the Phoenician alphabet.
   b. Roman spelling.
   c. the development of our alphabet.
   d. trading with foreign lands.

3. The word **their** in the first paragraph, last sentence, refers to

   _____.

4. The ancient Phoenicians developed a 26-character alphabet.

   Yes   No   Does not say

5. Which two sentences are not true?
   a. We use the Roman alphabet.
   b. The Greek alphabet was the first.
   c. The Semites had an alphabet.
   d. Hieroglyphics preceded alphabets.
   e. Written language was never really necessary.

6. What word in the second paragraph means **growing?** _____

Getting Ready to Read

Draw a line under each right answer or fill in the blank.

1. **Special activities** may be   **obsidian**   **ceremonies**   **froth.**

2. **So it seems** means   **bubbly**   **pumice**   **apparently.**

3. **Thick pieces** are   **spearheads**   **froth**   **chunks.**

4. **Ideas connected with a system of worship** are

                     ceremonies   **religious**   **obsidian.**

5. **Foam** may be called   **froth**   **bubbly**   **religious.**

6. **The action of a volcano** is _____.

H-9   Floating Rocks

Have you ever seen rocks float on water? Have you seen rocks blown through the air by the wind?

Pumice, which is a kind of rock that comes from volcanoes, is so light that it can float on water and can be carried long distances by wind. This rock resembles bubbly froth and is usually colored white, yellow, brown, or dull red. Small bits of pumice have been found as far as 130 kilometers (about 80 miles) from Oregon's Crater Lake, which once was a volcano. Apparently these bits of rock had been blown this distance by the wind. Some larger chunks of pumice from volcanic islands have been known to float on the ocean for as long as a year and a half.

Pumice is a variety of obsidian, or volcanic glass. Mostly black or gray in color, obsidian is harder than glass and can be broken into pieces that have thin, sharp edges, much like glass. The Native Americans chipped off pieces of obsidian to make knives, spearheads, and arrow points. Many of these tools were so highly valued that they were used as offerings to the gods in religious ceremonies.

H-9 Testing Yourself

NUMBER RIGHT

Draw a line under each right answer or fill in each blank.

1. While not directly stated, it can be reasoned from the article that
    a. heavy, solid objects do not float.   b. obsidian is costly.
    c. pumice is harder than glass.

2. This article as a whole is about
    a. Crater Lake.   c. the uses of obsidian.
    b. any volcanic rock.   d. one kind of volcanic rock.

3. The word **they** in the last sentence refers to _____.

4. Although pumice is light, it is very hard.   Yes   No   Does not say

5. Which two sentences are not true?
    a. Obsidian is a variety of pumice.   c. Glass is harder than obsidian.
    b. Pumice is a volcanic rock.   d. Native Americans used obsidian.
    e. Pumice is light enough to be carried by wind.

6. What word in the last paragraph means **things given as an act of worship?**

A Powerful Grin

In one of Colonel Davy Crockett's campaigns for election to the Congress of the United States, his opponent was a gentleman of polished manners who seldom spoke to an audience without wearing a broad smile during the entire speech. Noting the favorable effect of his opponent's grinning, the colonel made the following speech:

"Yes, gentlemen, my opponent may get some votes by grinning, for he can outgrin me—and you know I'm not slow when it comes to grinning. To prove that I'm not, let me tell you a story.

"You all know how much I love to hunt. Well, I discovered a long time ago that a 'coon couldn't stand my grin. With a grin, I can bring one tumbling from the highest tree. I never waste powder and lead when I want one of the creatures.

"Well, as I was walking out one night a few hundred yards from my house, I saw a 'coon planted upon one of the highest limbs of an old tree. The night was clear with a full moon, and my dog Rattler was with me. Rattler won't bark at a 'coon—he's a queer dog that way. So I decided to bring the varmint down in my usual way, with a grin.

"I set myself, and after grinning at the 'coon a reasonable time, I found that it didn't come down. I wondered why and took another steady grin at it. It still didn't come down. This made me a little mad, so I felt 'round and got an old branch about five feet long. I planted one end on the ground, placed my chin on the other end, and took a good rest. I then grinned my best for about five minutes. But the old 'coon hung on.

"Finding to my surprise that I could not bring it down by grinning, I went back to the house, got my axe, returned to the tree, saw the 'coon was still there, and began to cut away. Down came the tree, but there was no 'coon to be seen! I found that what I had taken for a 'coon was a large knot on the limb of the tree. And upon looking at it closely, I saw that I had grinned all the bark off and had left the knot perfectly smooth!

"Now, fellow citizens," continued Colonel Crockett, "you must be convinced that, in the grinning line, I myself am not exactly slow. Yet, when I look upon my opponent's face, I must admit that, in grinning, he is my superior. You must all admit it. Therefore, be wide awake. Do not let him grin you out of your votes."

MY READING TIME _____ **(450 WORDS)**

Thinking It Over

1. Is Davy Crockett telling his audience to vote for a person who smiles and is pleasant?

2. Do you think Crockett got most of the votes of the audience? What might they have liked best about him?

3. Do you think this would make a good campaign speech today? Give reasons for your answers.

Getting Ready to Read

fascinated

envied

indication

portend

newlyweds

omens

calamity

imitate

designs

whippoorwill

Draw a line under each right answer or fill in the blank.

1. **Very interested** means   **envied**   **fascinated**   **to imitate.**

2. It is a bird.   **portend**   **indication**   **whippoorwill**

3. **To give warning of** means **to**   **portend**   **envied**   **omens.**

4. **Signs of events that are about to happen** are called
                               portends   **designs**   **omens.**

5. **A calamity** means
                 good fortune   **disappointment**   **great misfortune.**

6. **People who have just been married** are called

_____.

I-1   Bird Luck

We have always been fascinated by birds. For ages before the airplane was invented, people envied birds in flight, and some even tried to imitate them. Many have

also considered birds as omens of good and bad luck.

For example, should a bird fly into your house, it would be an indication that important news is on the way. Should the bird be unable to find its way out, it would be a sign of death. Crows and hoot owls are generally considered to portend bad luck. A woodpecker tapping on a house is supposed to mean bad news. In addition, designs showing birds on wedding gifts have been considered bad luck because the happiness of the newlyweds will fly away.

On the other hand, barn swallows nesting in your barn or wrens building their nests near your house are signs of good fortune. Should you destroy a swallow's nest, however, calamity is sure to follow.

Some superstitions about birds do not involve good or bad luck. For instance, some people believe that the first time you hear a whippoorwill in spring you should note the time and place. You can count on being in the same place at the same time the following year.

I-1 Testing Yourself

Draw a line under each right answer or fill in each blank.

1. While not directly stated, it can be reasoned from the article that

    a. owls bring bad luck.   b. whippoorwills go south in winter.

    c. people's interest in flying brought about superstitions about birds.

2. This article as a whole is about

    a. superstitions about birds.   c. North American birds.

    b. facts about birds   d. woodpeckers bringing bad news.

3. The word **them** in the second sentence refers to _____.

4. Superstitions always involve good or bad luck.   Yes   No   Does not say

5. Which two sentences are not true?

    a. Crows are good omens.   c. Birds have been called omens.

    b. All birds are evil omens.   d. People have tried to imitate birds.

         e. We have always been interested in birds.

6. What word in the third paragraph means about the same as **ruin?**

165

Getting Ready to Read

medical	
plasma	
university	
degree	
liquid	
system	
deliver	
protest	
injure	

Draw a line under each right answer or fill in the blank.

1. It is **part of blood.**   medical   plasma   system

2. It means about the same as **college.**   university   system   degree

3. When you graduate from college, you get a
   degree   university   liquid.

4. It means the same as **to hurt.**   to protest   to deliver   to injure

5. Water is   **steam**   **a liquid**   **a solid.**

6. If I complain, I _____.

I-2   Blood of the Wrong Color?

Charles Drew was in the hospital. He had been hurt playing football. Drew admired the doctor's work on his leg. He decided to be a doctor also, even though he knew it would be difficult because he was black.

He worked hard to earn a medical degree from a Canadian university. He became interested in how to prevent injured persons from dying because of loss of blood. Persons who could give their own blood to the injured person often could not be found in time.

Drew searched for a better way. After much study, he found that the answer was plasma. Plasma is the liquid part of blood. It could be stored and used when needed.

Then came World War II. Charles Drew was put in charge of blood banks. He worked with the Red Cross to build a system to store and deliver the plasma.

At first, the Red Cross would not take blood given by black people. Drew protested. Finally, the Red Cross agreed. But they stored the plasma from black people separately.

In 1950, Drew was in an auto accident. He needed blood. But the nearest hospital was for whites only. He died before he could be taken to a hospital for blacks.

I-2   Testing Yourself

Draw a line under each right answer or fill in each blank.

1. While not directly stated, it can be reasoned from the article that
   a. some people thought blood from blacks was different from blood from whites.
   b. Charles Drew was an outstanding football player.
   c. people no longer die from loss of blood.

2. This article as a whole is about
   a. hospitals.
   b. becoming a doctor.
   c. how to treat injuries.
   d. the inventor of plasma storage.

3. The word **they** in the fifth paragraph, fourth sentence, refers to

   _____ _____.

4. The Red Cross no longer stores plasma from the blood of blacks separately from that of whites.   Yes   No   Does not say

5. Which two sentences are not true?
   a. Charles Drew was not allowed to become a doctor because he was black.
   b. Drew lived in Canada for a while.
   c. Drew lived during the time of World War II.
   d. Drew died after an auto accident.
   e. Plasma is the same as blood.

6. What word in the fourth paragraph means about the same as **a plan?**

   _____

Getting Ready to Read

alligators
dolphins
deadly
carnivorous
threat
wounded
protruding
sharklike
scent
fierce
twisting
piranha

Draw a line under each right answer or fill in the blank.

1. **An animal that eats meat** is said to be

   fierce   carnivorous   deadly.

2. **A smell** is **a   scent   dolphin   threat.**

3. **Sticking out** means   **sharklike   wounded   protruding.**

4. A road **turning sharply** is   **protruding   fierce   twisting.**

5. It means **very dangerous.   deadly   piranha   alligators**

6. **Hurt** or **injured** means _____.

I-3 A Deadly Fish

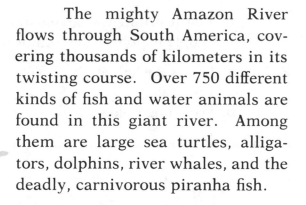

The mighty Amazon River flows through South America, covering thousands of kilometers in its twisting course. Over 750 different kinds of fish and water animals are found in this giant river. Among them are large sea turtles, alligators, dolphins, river whales, and the deadly, carnivorous piranha fish.

It is difficult to realize that a fish only about 30 centimeters (1 foot) long could be a threat to a large animal or to a human being. Yet the piranha fish, which is also called the *caribe*, is such a creature. Found in large numbers in the Amazon River, these fish will sometimes attack wounded people and animals in the water.

The fish travel in large groups, numbering sometimes in the thousands, and are equipped with strong, protruding lower jaws and double rows of sharklike teeth. They grow wild when the scent of blood from a wounded creature reaches them. Attacking their victim, they tear the body down to its bare skeleton in a matter of minutes.

The fierce piranhas may be divided into about 20 types. They are colored blue-gray, green, or yellow and have spots of red or gold.

I-3   Testing Yourself

NUMBER RIGHT

Draw a line under each right answer or fill in each blank.

1. While not directly stated, it can be reasoned from the article that
      a. piranhas will not attack when a person or animal is not hurt.
  b. piranhas attack only other fish.   c. piranhas make good food.

2. This article as a whole is about
    a. piranha fish.   c. fish of South America.
    b. the Amazon River.   d. the different types of piranhas.

3. The word **they** in the third paragraph, second sentence, refers to

                                 _____.

4. Piranha fish travel in groups.   Yes   No   Does not say

5. Which two sentences are not true?
    a. Some fish eat meat.   c. Piranhas attack wounded creatures.
    b. The Amazon is a short river.   d. Only piranhas are found in the Amazon.
          e. Piranha fish have protruding jaws.

6. What word in the second paragraph means about the same as **a danger?**

                                         _____

Getting Ready to Read

SAY AND KNOW

split

uranium

atomic

atoms

plutonium

arrival

scarce

determine

alternative

Draw a line under each right answer or fill in the blank.

1. **To divide** means **to   split   atom   determine.**

2. **Easy to get** is **the opposite of   atomic   plutonium   scarce.**

3. Reaching a place is one's   **uranium   arrival   alternative.**

4. **To settle** or **decide** is **to   determine   split   scarce.**

5. **The smallest bits of a chemical substance** are called
                                              plutoniums   atoms   splits.

6. **One of two things that can be chosen for a certain purpose** is an

_____.

I-4   Better than Gold

Gold and silver are not the only precious metals that people have valued. In the middle of the twentieth century, a metal called *uranium* was sought by scientists and fortune hunters.

Uranium actually was discovered in 1789. Not until the arrival of the atomic age, however, was its value fully known. The metal became very important when it was discovered that uranium atoms could be split and used to develop atomic energy.

There is more than one kind of uranium. At first, it was only the scarce element called U235 that could be used for creating atomic energy. The much more common element U238 could not be used as an alternative for this important purpose. Later, a way of making a chemical called plutonium from U238 was found. The plutonium atoms could then be split to create atomic power.

Uranium has been of use to us not only in producing atomic energy, but also in helping scientists determine the age of Earth. Scientists discovered that uranium in time turns to lead, and they found ways of determining just how long it takes for this change to occur. By studying rocks that contain both uranium and lead, scientists have been able to discover that Earth is at least 4½ billion years old.

I-4   Testing Yourself

Draw a line under each right answer or fill in each blank.

1. While not directly stated, it can be reasoned from the article that
   a. scientists can now manufacture uranium.
   b. whole atoms do not produce atomic energy.
   c. uranium had great value in 1789.

2. This article as a whole is about
   a. gold, silver, and uranium.
   b. uranium and plutonium.
   c. uranium.
   d. finding the age of Earth.

3. The word **its** in paragraph two refers to _____.

4. Uranium turns to lead after two thousand years.   Yes   No   Does not say

5. Which two sentences are not true?
   a. Earth is 6 billion years old.
   b. Scientists can produce atomic energy.
   c. Uranium is valuable.
   d. Gold has never been valued.
   e. Scientists can split atoms.

6. What word in the fourth paragraph means **making?** _____

Getting Ready to Read

Draw a line under each right answer or fill in the blank.

magazines

dwellings

purchase

absolutely

civilization

Arabs

practically

material

soaked

pulp

1. **Places to live** are   **magazines   pulp   dwellings.**

2. **Almost** means   **absolutely   practically   soaked.**

3. It is **a publication with stories and articles.**

    magazine   Arabs   material

4. It means **buy.   soaked   purchase   pulp**

5. **The culture of a people** is **their**

    magazine   civilization   material.

6. Something that is **thoroughly wet** is _____ .

I-5 Paper, Paper, Everywhere

Wherever we look around us, we find paper. It is used in our books, in our newspapers, and in our magazines. Paper is used in the walls and roofs of our dwellings. Some of the goods we purchase at stores are wrapped in paper. In short, paper seems to be absolutely necessary to our modern civilization. It is hard to believe that there was a time when people did not have it.

In 4000 B.C., the Egyptians first made a sort of paper from the papyrus plant. Historians believe, however, that true paper was probably first invented by the Chinese. The knowledge of this discovery gradually spread over the world and was brought into Europe by the Arabs in the eighth century.

Paper can be made out of practically any vegetable material that contains fibers. Rags were first used; they were cleaned, soaked, boiled, and reduced to pulp by heating and grinding. The pulp was then placed between pieces of felt, rolled thin, and dried. Today most paper is made by machinery out of wood pulp.

More than 85 percent of all waste materials recycled in the United States each year are paper products. Twenty-five percent of all U.S. paper is recycled.

I-5   Testing Yourself

NUMBER RIGHT

Draw a line under each right answer or fill in each blank.

1. While not directly stated, it can be reasoned from the article that
    a. our civilization would be very different without paper.
    b. no one has ever had a civilization without paper.
    c. paper is becoming less important to us.

2. This article as a whole is about
    a. an article of clothing.
    b. how paper is used.
    c. different kinds of paper.
    d. paper.

3. The word **they** in the third paragraph refers to _____.

4. Rags have been used for making paper.   Yes   No   Does not say

5. Which two sentences are not true?
    a. Paper is used in building houses.
    b. Paper must be made of wood pulp.
    c. True paper may have come from China.
    d. Paper is made of vegetable matter.
    e. Europeans brought paper to the Arabs in 800.

6. What word in the second paragraph means about the same as **slowly?**

Getting Ready to Read

SAY AND KNOW

reveal
favorable
obviously
increase
calculate
consequently
combination
pattern
accurately

Draw a line under each right answer or fill in the blank.

1. **A set of two or more things** is a   reveal   combination   favorable.

2. It means **quite clearly.**   obviously   pattern   increase

3. **To grow larger** is to   reveal   pattern   increase.

4. It is about the same as **a plan.**   consequently   accurately   pattern

5. It means **as a result.**   consequently   favorable   accurately

6. It means about the same as **to figure out.** _____

I-6 True-False

Have you ever wondered how well you could do on a true-false test if you simply guessed on every question?

You know that on a one-question test your chances would be even. There are only two possible answers: T or F. Consequently, you have as much chance of being right as wrong.

What about a two-question test? First, calculate how many possible sets of answers there are. The two questions could both be true, or they could both be false. Or, they could be true and false, or false and true. Therefore, there are four possible combinations.

With three questions, the number of possible sets of answers increases to eight. Here they are: TTT, TTF, TFT, TFF, FTT, FTF, FFT, and FFF. Obviously, your chances of guessing right on three questions are less favorable.

How many possible sets of answers are there in a four-question test? If you have calculated it accurately, you will know there are 16.

Perhaps this table will reveal a pattern. How many combinations of answers could there be for five questions?

Questions	Sets of Answers
1	2
2	4
3	8
4	16

174

Most tests, however, are longer than five questions. Do you know how many possible sets of answers there are in a 20-question test? 1,048,576!

I-6 Testing Yourself

Draw a line under each right answer or fill in each blank.

1. While not directly stated, it can be reasoned from the article that
   a. a 40-question true-false test would have twice as many possible sets of answers as a 20-question true-false test.
   b. the fewer the questions, the better your chances of guessing right.
   c. it would be impossible to guess right for all the answers of a four-question true-false test.

2. This article as a whole is about
   a. true-false tests.
   b. true-false test answers.
   c. chances of guessing right on true-false tests.
   d. how to make good true-false questions.

3. The word **they** in the third paragraph, third sentence, refers to

   _____ _____ .

4. You have an even chance if you guess the answer to a one-question true-false test.

   Yes   No   Does not say

5. Which two sentences are not true?
   a. A 20-question true-false test has over a million possible sets of answers.
   b. Every time the questions increase by one, the sets of possible answers get twice as large.
   c. There are two possible answers for a one-question true-false test.
   d. A three-question true-false test has four times as many sets of possible answers as a two-question test.
   e. Your chances of guessing right on a four-question true-false test are one in eight.

6. What word in the fifth paragraph, second sentence, means the same as **correctly?**

   _____

Getting Ready to Read

SAY AND KNOW

triangle
spiral
persuade
sightseer
expose
geometrical
reptile
suggestion
unusual

Draw a line under each right answer or fill in the blank.

1. **A three-sided figure** is **a**   triangle   sightseer   reptile.

2. **To uncover** is **to**   suggest   persuade   expose.

3. Snakes and lizards are   **geometrical   spiral   reptiles.**

4. **Something out of the ordinary** is

   expose   unusual   suggestion.

5. It is **like a coil.**   spiral   sightseer   triangle

6. One who looks at scenery is a _____.

I-7   A Giant Artist?

"A huge giant must have drawn those pictures!" This is what you might think if you were looking down from an airplane near Nazca, Peru.

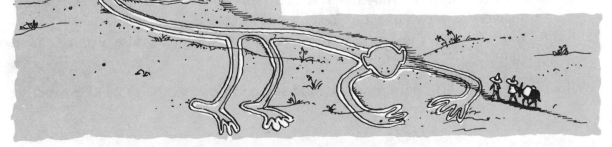

On the rainless land below, you would see triangles, spirals, and other geometrical figures. You would also see flowers, birds, whales, reptiles, and monkeys. One drawing of a monkey is longer than a football field.

The drawings were probably made by the Nazca people about 1900 years ago. They picked up stones, piling them in rows, exposing the lighter earth beneath.

Why they did this is a puzzle. The drawings can be recognized only from the air. Yet the Nazcas had no way to view them from above.

For some time, Maria Reiche, a mathematician, has been making a map of all these Nazca Lines. She is amazed at how straight some of the lines are. They stretch several kilometers, descending into valleys and over hills, always in a straight line.

One suggestion is that these lines marked landing fields for space visitors. Reiche says no. The ground is soft. Space visitors would have become stuck.

These unusual lines are now in danger of being stamped out by sightseers. Reiche has persuaded Peru to try to protect the ancient markings.

I-7 Testing Yourself

NUMBER RIGHT

Draw a line under each right answer or fill in each blank.

1. While not directly stated, it can be reasoned from the article that
    a. the Nazcas had a good system for making straight lines.
    b. the Nazcas thought of whales and monkeys as gods.
    c. the Nazcas must have had balloons to help them do the drawings.

2. This article as a whole is about
    a. a giant artist.
    b. a mathematician.
    c. visitors from outer space.
    d. mysterious drawings.

3. The word **them** in the third paragraph, second sentence, refers to

    _____.

4. No visitors from outer space have ever landed on Earth.

    Yes   No   Does not say

5. Which two sentences are not true?
    a. Maria Reiche makes maps of the Nazca Lines.
    b. Some of the drawings are of birds.
    c. The Nazcas made the drawings about 1900 years ago.
    d. The Nazcas used oil paints for the lines.
    e. Heavy rains fall in Nazca, Peru.

6. What word in the last sentence means about the same as **to save?**

    _____

Getting Ready to Read

Draw a line under each right answer or fill in the blank.

vowel

international

phonetic

experts

standard

confusing

improved

acquired

incorporating

meaningful

1. A new possession has been

    incorporated   acquired   improved.

2. It refers to all speech sounds.   **standard   vowel   phonetic**

3. **Grown better** is   **confusing   phonetic   improved.**

4. **Making something a part of something else** is

    international   confusing   incorporating.

5. **A model** or **rule** is   **a vowel   a standard   an expert.**

6. **Something that mixes you up** is called _____.

I-8   Alpha and Beta

The alphabet invented by the Phoenicians contained only consonants. The Greeks improved upon the written language that they acquired from the Phoenicians by incorporating five vowel sounds. By about 800 B.C., the Greeks had built up an alphabet of 24 letters, including the five vowels. The first two letters in the Greek alphabet were called *alpha* and *beta*, and these were combined to form the word *alphabet*.

The next meaningful change in the history of the alphabet was made by another great people, the Romans, whose language was called Latin. The Romans adopted the Greek alphabet, perfected it, and passed it on to later people. Today, almost every European language is written with the Roman alphabet.

Although people who speak and write English use the Roman alphabet, it is not the ideal way to record the English language. This is also true of some other languages that use the Roman alphabet. Scholars have tried to solve this problem by devising an 80-character alphabet called the International Phonetic Alphabet. In this alphabet, experts have made up standard letters or symbols for sounds that may be confusing when expressed in Roman letters.

I-8 Testing Yourself

Draw a line under each right answer or fill in each blank.

1. While not directly stated, you can tell from the article that
      a. a proper English alphabet would use more characters than the Roman one.
      b. the Roman alphabet has too many characters.
      c. the International Phonetic Alphabet is used in the United Nations.

2. This article as a whole is about
      a. the Greek alphabet.   c. the development of the alphabet.
      b. modern languages.   d. the Romans' use of Semitic words.

3. The word **these** in paragraph one refers to _____.

4. The English use the Roman alphabet.   Yes   No   Does not say

5. Which two sentences are not true?
      a. The Greek alphabet has only consonants.
      b. The Greek alphabet had 24 letters.
      c. The Latin alphabet was based upon the Greek alphabet.
      d. Alpha is the name of the first letter in the Greek alphabet.
      e. The Phoenicians added consonants to the Greek alphabet.

6. What word in the last paragraph means **perfect?** _____

Getting Ready to Read

SAY AND KNOW | Draw a line under each right answer or fill in the blank.

reservation

famous

officially

performance

magical

replied

immediate

solo

chorus

1. A group of people singing together is

                         famous   a chorus   a reservation.

2. It means **right now.**   replied   performance   immediate

3. If you are **well known,** you are   famous   magical   solo.

4. It means **a place where many Native Americans live.**

                                   reservation   solo   chorus

5. When you **perform alone,** you **do it**   together   immediate   solo.

6. Something done formally is **done** _____.

I-9   The Firebird

Can you jump high enough to beat your feet together twice before coming down? Maria Tallchief could. In fact, this Osage Native American dancer could beat her feet together eight times!

Tallchief was born on a reservation in Oklahoma. She took dancing lessons when she was young. To get the best teachers, her family moved to Los Angeles when she was eight. Later they moved to New York. Maria Tallchief was hired by a famous dance company, the Ballet Russe.

She danced in the chorus at first. But she studied solo parts.

She made herself ready in case a solo dancer became ill. Then, when she was 18, she danced her first solo part. She was an immediate hit. The newspapers called her the "Dancing Osage" and the "Indian Princess." Tallchief replied that she was proud of being Native American, but she was not a princess.

180

Her best performance was as the Firebird, a beautiful wild bird with magical powers. She soon became famous all over the world. In 1953, the people in her home town, Fairfax, Oklahoma, put on a Maria Tallchief Day. After a feast of Native American foods, an Osage chief officially made her a princess. So she finally became a princess after all.

I-9 Testing Yourself

NUMBER RIGHT

Draw a line under each right answer or fill in each blank.

1. While not directly stated, it can be reasoned from the article that
   a. no other dancer could jump as high as Maria Tallchief.
   b. Tallchief was determined to be a solo dancer.
   c. Tallchief would have succeeded even without lessons.

2. This article as a whole is about
   a. the Osage Native Americans. c. a Native American dancer.
   b. the Ballet Russe. d. Maria Tallchief Day.

3. The word **they** in the second paragraph, fourth sentence, refers to

   _____

4. Maria Tallchief was not born a princess.   Yes   No   Does not say

5. Which two sentences are not true?
   a. Maria Tallchief lived in Los Angeles when young.
   b. Tallchief danced solo as soon as she arrived in New York.
   c. Tallchief was an Iroquois.
   d. Tallchief became best known as the Firebird.
   e. Tallchief came from a town in Oklahoma.

6. What word in the last paragraph means **a great meal with lots to eat and drink?**

   _____

Wanted: $12,000 Reward

"Tie him up!" The overseer, whip in hand, waited for 15-year-old Harriet Tubman to do as she was ordered. But just then, the young slave who was to be punished broke free and ran.

Quickly the overseer picked up an iron weight. He threw it at the escaping slave. But his aim was poor. Harriet, standing nearby, was struck in the head.

For months she lay in bed. Death was near. Somehow she recovered, but for the rest of her life she would occasionally fall into a stupor. At such times, she seemed out of her mind. People thought her to be half-witted.

Although this incident nearly cost Harriet Tubman her life, it also later helped to save it. At the time, she was one of eleven children in a slave family in Maryland. As a slave, she did not go to school.

Every day she dreamed of freedom. Then one day in 1849, she escaped, starting north by herself.

She traveled mostly by night. She used the North Star to guide her. On cloudy nights, when the stars could not be seen, she felt for moss on tree trunks. She knew moss grew on the north side of trees, the shady side.

The Underground Railroad also helped her. This was not really a railroad. It was also not underground. It was actually a secret organization of people who helped slaves escape from the South to the North and freedom.

At last, Harriet Tubman reached Philadelphia safely. She found a job as a house servant. Then her thoughts turned to her family, still slaves in the South. She knew she would have to go back and help them escape too.

Before she was through, Harriet Tubman helped not only her family but also about 300 others to escape. She learned many helpful tricks. Sometimes it helped while in the South to pretend to be half-witted as a result of the blow to her head when she was young. She also carried along a live chicken. Sometimes when she saw danger ahead, she let the chicken go. She then chased it madly. The people watching laughed at the frantic efforts of this poor old lady to catch the chicken. In the meantime, her party of escaping slaves went on unnoticed.

Harriet Tubman became a well-known "conductor" of the Underground Railroad. The slaves whom she led called her "Moses." A reward of $12,000 in gold was offered by law officers for her capture. But she was never caught.

During the Civil War, Harriet was of great help to the North. She was a nurse. She was also a spy. Once she led a company of 300 black soldiers in a raid that freed nearly 800 slaves.

MY READING TIME _____ (450 WORDS)

Thinking It Over

1. Why was Harriet Tubman given the name "Moses" by slaves?

2. Was Harriet Tubman really "half-witted"? Give reasons for your answer.

3. Why were slaves not sent to school?

Keeping Track of Growth

Study this sample graph. To record the score for Unit A, put a dot on the line beside the number which tells how often Question 4 was answered correctly. Do the same for Units B, C, and so on. Draw a line to join the dots. The line will show how this reading skill is growing.

Notice that each graph records the progress made on one question. See how this reader improved in answering Question 4 in each unit except Unit E.

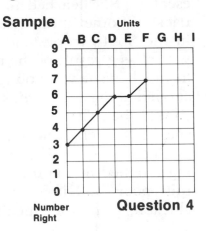

Sample

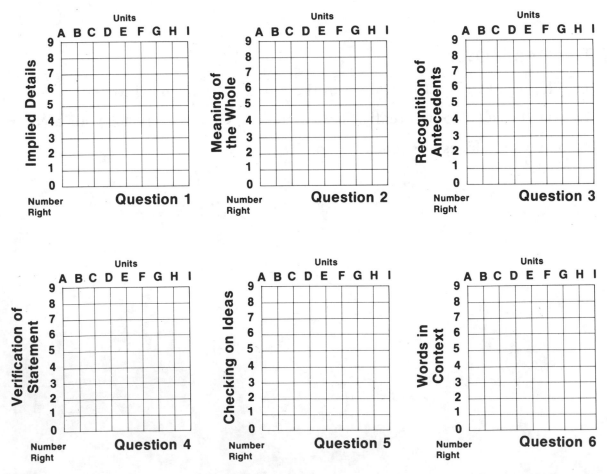

186